Make-Up Their Mind

MAKE-UP THEIR MIND

Mind Aesthetics®

Methods and Techniques to Persuade
and Influence Your Clients
and Make Them Feel Beautiful, Inside

Dr. Julian Cauceglia

Copyright © 2002 Dr. Julian A. Cauceglia
All rights reserved

No part of this book may be used or reproduced or copied or distributed in any form, or by any means, or stored in a database or retrieval system, or displayed on the internet without prior written permission of the author.

Mind Aesthetics® is a registered trademark.

Published by Pegasus Publishing, Fort Myers, FL

Cover Design by Jonathan Gullery

Printed in USA

ISBN 0-9717407-1-2

Library of Congress Card Number: 2002092894

Dedication

For my loving wife Ivette.

Your boundless support,
encouragement and tolerance
is the foundation of my achievement.

You have shown me what true beauty really is.

Table Of Contents

Introduction 1
1. Beauty 5
2. The Human Mind 9
3. Representational Systems 13
4. Submodalities 27
5. Sensory Acuity 29
6. Mind Aesthetics® 35
7. Zone Exercise 43
8. Rapport 61
9. Reading The Client - Representational Types 67
10. Eye Accessing Cues 87
11. Representational System Pacing 91
12. Mirroring and Matching 97
13. Verbal Pacing 109
14. Other Pacing Methods 117
15. Calibration and Leading 121
16. The Magic 125
17. Formulating Effective Suggestions 133
18. The Mind Aesthetics® 141
19. Ethics 147
Appendix A 149
Index 163
Bibliography 165
Mind Aesthetics® CD Order Form 167

Introduction

Mind Aesthetics® represents an innovative new approach to the field of beauty that will assist you in improving the quality of your services, while providing the client with a new and wonderful experience when they visit your salon or spa. Mind Aesthetics® is a unique concept, a hybrid based on years of my own research, development and study, which gives appropriate credit to its roots: Neuro Linguistic Programming or NLP, (the study of the structure of subjective experience, behavior and communication, with theories, techniques, presuppositions and methods that produce models of excellence based on how individuals structure their experience) developed by Richard Bandler and John Grinder, and the relaxation and suggestion characteristics of hypnosis (a completely natural and normal state of heightened relaxation and acute sensory perception that bypasses our conscious mind and critical factor, opening our subconscious mind
to direct input, creating increased suggestibility).

    The first few chapters of this book are designed to provide the minimum basic understanding of these studies, as you will need them to properly use the Mind Aesthetics® techniques. They contain a lot of important information that you will use later, so spend all the time you need to become well acquainted with the background.

Mind Aesthetics® has two primary facets. The first involves techniques you can use while interacting with your client, which equip you with the tools necessary to:

1. Increase the value of your existing services, enabling you to increase the amount of revenue you receive in exchange for them.

2. Create a strong, indelible bond between you and your clients, causing them to become and remain frequent, repeat customers.

3. Actually suggest directly to your client's subconscious mind that they should purchase products and services, tell others about their wonderful experience, and encourage their friends to visit you . . . and believe it was their own idea!

4. Make you the most requested individual in your salon or spa.

5. Cause your client to truly look and feel beautiful from the inside - where true beauty begins.

As you develop and refine these skills, they will help you realize an increase in repeat business and referrals and give you an enormous advantage in your ability to influence your clients and persuade them to purchase products and services while remaining loyal, repeat customers, who will feel compelled to tell others about you, and encourage them to visit you.

The second facet of Mind Aesthetics® benefits your client directly, by providing them with a uniquely positive experience, unlike anything they may have come to expect in a salon or spa. Properly used, the Mind Aesthetics® techniques and CD will instill within the client an

Introduction

overwhelmingly positive energy that will dynamically enhance the physical sensations of your services or treatments, while dramatically increasing the actual benefit they receive from them on all sensory levels, simultaneously relaxing them more than ever before. Then, with their body and mind now properly prepared, they are guided to a depth of relaxation that opens their subconscious mind and they are made to feel beautiful, on the inside, from the deepest subconscious level. Furthermore, they are instilled with the feeling of both literal, physical beauty, and the deeper understanding of the subconscious concept of being beautiful. They are filled with positive energy that will remain with them, making them feel beautiful, both inside and out. Thus, your services take on a unique and improved quality while your clients realize benefits that, until now, could only be dreamed of.

This is Mind Aesthetics®.

1
Beauty

Although Mind Aesthetics® is designed to improve your bottom line through persuasion, influence and proper interaction with the client, we must maintain a clear vision of its primary objective: improving the client's physical and mental state and instilling within them the feeling of being beautiful inside. However, before we begin to discuss the various facets of Mind Aesthetics®, it is necessary that first we discuss beauty itself, in order to gain some background and share a common perspective. Let us consider mankind's timeless obsession with this thing we call *beauty*.

The human quest for beauty is as old as civilization itself, and, in some of us, it is as basic a drive as any other instinct. The oldest records of mankind's development contain references and indications of ornate decorations and other efforts utilized in an attempt to make people appear more attractive. Archeological research in ancient Egypt has revealed a culture in which physical beauty was of paramount importance. The art of the time depicts men as slim, well-built and muscular with broad shoulders, and women as having small waists, with well-exercised midriffs, flat stomachs and full breasts. Those of means decorated themselves with gems and gold in an effort to become even more attractive. Wealthy and poor alike used perfumes (scented oils were provided as part of the wages of the less wealthy), and there is indisputable evidence of a wide variety of makeup in many colors, with particular attention given to the eyes. Hair was colored or covered with wigs, dyed in every imaginable color, including green, blue, gold and, of course, blonde, and elaborate hair-clips, pins and combs were common. Ancient Egyptian chemists are known to have developed formulas to reduce or remove stretch marks in women, and to promote the growth of hair in men.

The Ancient Egyptians were not alone. Ancient Greek women had their hair styled with elegant ornamentation, using elaborate combs to enhance their appearance. Cosmetics derived from natural herbs, plants and minerals were used to whiten skin, redden the cheeks, and blacken the eyebrows. Proper hygiene was an important aspect of beauty, with frequent baths and a ritualization of cleanliness that included the washing of feet and rub-downs of oil.

Ancient Roman men and woman were also preoccupied with physical appearance. Both wore make-up and perfume to enhance their physical attraction to the opposite sex and sometimes to same-sex love interests. Jewelry was also a very common adornment in all cultures.

The Aztec and Mayan civilizations also shared this preoccupation with beauty, and, although they were on the other side of the world, their idea of beauty and their efforts to achieve it were curiously similar to those of the Egyptians, Greeks and Romans.

It is also worth noting that each of the cultures mentioned above, as well as many others, had a god and/or goddess who reigned over beauty and represented the ideal that all men and woman strove to attain.

Certainly, mankind's quest for beauty still exists today. When we consider the many industries, from clothing to cars, from surgery to jewelry, which have their finger in the multi-billion dollar a year business of beauty, we see that, if anything, it is more pronounced than ever before.

We may ask ourselves why this obsession with beauty exists. Undoubtedly the answer can be found in our most primitive need to survive and procreate. All living creatures share the drive to further their kind. Even our earliest ancestors selected their mates with the continuance of the species as their instinctual, primary goal. Males sought females who appeared to be the best breeders, able to bear healthy offspring and care for them properly, and females chose healthy, strong men, using the abilities to provide and protect as criteria in selecting their mates. These very characteristics made one attractive, or *beautiful*, to the other, and these same qualities evolved into our modern-day definition of what is *beautiful*. Thus the desire to be beautiful is deeply rooted in our very need to survive.

However, I believe that there is another ever-present need that drives our desire to be beautiful, which is every bit as powerful as our instinct to survive. To understand it, we must first understand the basic functioning of the human mind.

2
The Human Mind

Consider the following statement:

"Beauty is more than skin deep."

Now, we have all heard this somewhat cliched phrase. However, have we ever really thought about what it means? In fact, this statement is more profound then it may first appear. Let us explore why.

To appreciate the real meaning of the statement, we must explore the inner workings of the human mind, and its relationship to the physical body.

Our mind can be thought of as being divided into two major parts: the conscious mind and the subconscious mind. In our computer age, we can analogize the two parts of the mind to a computer model by considering the subconscious mind as the hardware of the computer; storing, processing and remembering information, and the conscious mind as the software which uses the hardware (the subconscious mind) to accomplish its tasks (day to day existence), while being unable to operate without it.

This is not to imply that we have two minds. We do

not. The mind is a single, unified whole. However, two very distinct levels do exist, each with specific and unique functions and responsibilities.

The subconscious mind contains and controls our emotions, feelings, creativity, curiosity, memories, habits and what we have learned from each of our experiences. The subconscious mind is also responsible for all of the involuntary functions that keep us alive, such as respiration, digestion, circulation, elimination, hormones, nerve responses, survival, etc., as well as our involuntary muscle movements. This is perhaps the most important function of the subconscious mind, its ability to automatically control all of our bodily functions. A direct result of this automation is the power our subconscious programming has to directly affect our health, both physical and emotional.

The subconscious is the dominant part of our mind, encompassing 95% or more of our mind throughout our entire lives. However, despite its size and power, the vast majority of us are not even aware of its existence.

At the time of our birth, only the subconscious mind exists, as the conscious mind has not yet developed. Even before we are born, the subconscious mind is active and working, absorbing information, directing our lives, and forming beliefs from within the womb.

Once we enter the world, our subconscious mind continues to absorb information without criticizing its content, accuracy or validity. It simply accepts everything that is experienced as true and valid, and retains the memory and teaching of that experience as a series of beliefs. This is why we say children are "impressionable": all offered input is uncritically accepted.

The subconscious mind is literal, and does not distinguish between negative and positive. Consequently, it does not demonstrate rational behavior, but accepts all sensory input as fact. Once an idea has entered the subconscious, it is immediately accepted, recorded and reacted to accordingly, and forever, unless or until some influence changes or amends the existing belief. It is only then that the new programming becomes the unquestioned belief. This characteristic of the subconscious is the source of all of the good and bad we realize throughout our lives. Beliefs are retained and habits followed by the subconscious without specific concern for the effect they may ultimately have on us, nor is any consideration ever given to the source of the information, whether it is negative or positive, or its validity.

Our subconscious mind then implements all of our thoughts and ideas, taking control of our lives and directing every detail and function, internal and external, which we will ultimately experience. It does not take the time to analyze a situation; it reacts, immediately. It has a complete understanding of every capability of the human body as a mechanism, and how to make it function at its peak. Our subconscious mind is able to control every aspect of our life right down to the atomic level, even to the point of being able to change the growth and production of cells within the body.

Every single iota of sensory input that we experience in our lives is retained in the subconscious mind. It stores each and every experience as an image, sound, feeling, taste, or smell. It has a memory capacity in excess of 100 trillion images, far more than we can use in several lifetimes. This is why we only use a small portion of our brain capacity. Our subconscious mind encodes billions and billions of impressions as encoded data, in much the same way as a computer digitizes a photograph, making the storage and retrieval of this data remarkably efficient. Although our conscious mind sleeps when we do, our subconscious mind never sleeps, remaining alert and active every moment of our lives, keeping us alive by controlling all of our involuntary muscles and functions, and responding continually to all input, internal and external. Even as our conscious mind retreats, the subconscious is still open, recording the sensory input of every second of our lives.

3
Representational Systems

A better understanding of ourselves will give us the tools we need when interacting with our clients. Everything we experience originates as input from our senses. That input is then encoded and recorded in our subconscious minds for reference and consideration. Consequently, we communicate our *representation* of the world in the language of our five senses. We can associate our *representational systems* to their corresponding senses as seen in Fig. 1.

It is important for us to understand what representational system is dominant in the client to structure communication to their subconscious mind so as to ensure the best possible understanding. Our dominant representational system is not static, it is dynamic. This means that it will change according to the circumstances present during the input and output of information. It therefore becomes useful for us to expand our skills, enhancing the recognition and use of all representational systems whenever possible. This will give us a better, more comprehensive understanding of how we and our clients

SENSE	REPRESENTATIONAL SYSTEM
SIGHT	VISUAL
HEARING	AUDITORY
FEELING	KINESTHETIC
SMELL	OLFACTORY
TASTE	GUSTATORY

Fig. 1: Representational Systems

process sensory input as information, thus improving our ability to communicate and influence.

One way in which we can determine the dominant representational system being used at any given time is simply by listening to the words chosen when speaking. We all include words that correspond to the representational system that we are using at the time, without consciously realizing it.

For example, you may hear a person make a statement such as, "This looks like a good place to stop." If we study this statement, we find that the word *look* is used by the speaker. This illustrates the use of his or her visual representational system, as looking is related
to the sense of sight.

Other examples include:

Auditory: "*Sounds* like a good idea to me."
Kinesthetic: "Something doesn't *feel* right about that."
Olfactory: "This whole thing *stinks*."
Gustatory: "I am so mad I can *taste* it."

In the United States, as in most western cultures, we are more apt to use the first three representational systems, visual, auditory, and kinesthetic. This is because our society is such that we seldom think in terms of smell or taste, those representational systems dominate less frequently. Eastern cultures, on the other hand, utilize their gustatory and olfactory representational systems to a much greater extent. However, anyone can use any or all of the above systems during any given experience.

The words we use which indicate which representational system we are currently using are known as *predicates*. They are usually verbs, adverbs or adjectives. For illustrative purposes, Fig. 2 provides examples of commonly used predicates (this is a very limited list, just to help you to understand the concept).

Identifying and understanding representational systems is an essential part of utilizing them to our advantage. The exercise below will assist you in determining your own dominant representational system and presents a useful opportunity for you to practice and develop the technique. This is a skill you will use every day when interacting with your clients, and even beyond that, with your family, friends, and everyone in your social and professional environments. As with any new, learned skill, the more you practice
the more it will become part of your normal, natural routine.

Read the following questions and the accompanying answers. Quickly select the very first answer that comes to mind. Avoid second guessing

Visual	Auditory	Kinesthetic	Olfactory	Gustatory
see	sound	feel	smell	taste
picture	hear	relax	fragrant	sweet
imagine	listen	grasp	stink	sour
notice	quiet	touch	stench	bitter
look	talk	hold	musty	tasty
eye	shout	pressure	pungent	yummy
appear	din	smooth	reek	swallow
clear	noisy	hot	aroma	delicious
dark	volume	cold	snuff	zesty
colorful	loud	firm	scent	spicy
hazy	whisper	soothed	fresh	savory
observe	articulate	ouch	sniff	relish
visualize	scream	sharp	odor	luscious
focus	ring-a-bell	peaceful	musky	nauseating

Fig. 2: Representational System Predicates

yourself, or extensive thought or analysis. Your first, instinctive response will usually be the correct one. If you are unable to make a selection between two answers, select the one that appears first. If you are unable to choose between all three, then reread the question, recall an experience from your past that emulates it and determine how you reacted in that situation.

There are no correct or incorrect answers, as there is no one representational system that is preferable to another. The purpose of this exercise is simply to identify your dominant representational system and help to develop and refine the skill of identifying it in others.

1. **Recall a time when you found yourself very attracted to someone. What was the first thing that attracted you to them?**
A. How they looked.
B. Something they said or some other sound they made.
C. Your reaction to their touch or the way they made you feel.
D. Their perfume or scent.
E. A particular taste that you associated with them.

2. **When you especially enjoy a meal, what do you notice first?**
A. The colors and shapes of the food.
B. The sounds associated with it being prepared.
C. The temperature and/or texture of the food, or the atmosphere of the place in which you are eating.
D. The smell of the food.
E. The actual taste of the food.

3. **Thinking back to a memorable event, what is the first thing you recall?**
A. A visual image of the event.
B. The sounds associated with that event.
C. How the event made you feel.
D. The fragrances or scents associated with the event.
E. The taste of food, drink, etc. related to that event.

4. **When you drive, to determine where you are going, do you:**
A. Refer to a map or observe road signs.
B. Follow specific sounds that lead you to your destination.
C. Rely on your gut, or in other words, how you "feel" you should go.
D. Utilize your sense of smell to direct you.
E. Lick or bite your lips or stick your tounge out as you concentrate on where to go.

5. **Think about eating a carrot. What appeals to you first?**
A. Its color.
B. The way it sounds when you bite it.
C. The texture of its flesh.
D. Its smell.
E. Its taste.

6. **When you engage in your favorite sport, what do you enjoy most?**
A. The way you imagine you look playing it.
B. The sounds of the game.

Representational Systems

    C. The way the tools of the game feel, such as the grip of the club, or the sense of motion associated with the sport.
    D. The smell of sweat or other scents associated with the sport, such as the smell of racing car fuel.
    E. Some taste associated with the sport, such as a salty taste in your mouth.

7. Do you find instructions easier to understand when:
A. They are written and you can read them.
B. Someone explains them to you.
C. You jump right in and begin to follow them, like when you assemble a bicycle.
D. You are aware of pleasant scents in the air.
E. You are eating or drinking something.

8. When you are angered would you say you:
A. See red.
B. Listen to reason.
C. Breathe fire.
D. Think it stinks.
E. Can just spit.

9. When you are solving a problem do you:
A. Write it down to see it more clearly.
B. Talk it out, either to yourself or others.
C. Think about all possible aspects until you feel you have developed a solution.
E. Light a cigarette or find a scent in some other way that helps to focus you.
F. Get something to eat or drink.

Make-Up Their Mind

10. When engaging in sex do you:
A. Like to have the lights on so you can see everything that is going on.
B. Close your eyes and listen to the sounds.
C. Notice only the sensations and physical feeling.
D. Find the scent arousing.
E. Savor the flavor of a kiss or the taste of your partner's skin.

11. When purchasing clothing do you:
A. Picture yourself in the outfit.
B. Listen to the sales clerk or discuss the pros and cons of buying it with yourself.
C. Touch the material and imagine how you would feel wearing it.
D. Smell the material.
E. Imagine yourself wearing the outfit while going out to dinner or having a drink.

12. You classify people by:
A. The way they look.
B. The way they sound.
C. The way they feel or make you feel.
D. The way they smell.
E. By describing their personality as a flavor (sweet, sour, etc.)

13. Which of the following groups do you tend to favor?
A. Movies, photography, painting, reading.
B. Music, the sound of waves on the beach, the wind, chimes, thunder.
C. Massages, facials, craft work, kinetic art, petting your dog or cat.

D. Perfume, incense, scented candles, the smell of the air after rain.
E. The taste of wine or fine cognac, strong spices, a lollipop, an ice cream cone.

14. When recalling a previous lover, the *first* thing you do is:
A. See an image of the person.
B. Hear their voice.
C. Get a feeling (good or bad) inside.
D. Smell their perfume or cologne.
E. Sense the taste of them in your mouth.

15. Recall a time when you were horseback riding or hiking. What do you recall first?
A. An image or picture of the trail.
B. The sound of you or the horse walking.
C. The temperature of the air or the feel of the horse's motion.
D. The smell of the air or the horse.
E. The taste of the dust in your mouth.

16. If you encounter someone you dislike when do you first notice them?
A. As they approach.
B. When they speak.
C. When they get close to you.
D. When you smell them.
E. When you observe them eating or drinking something.

17. When you go to bed at night, it is important that:
A. The room is dark.
B. It is very quiet.
C. The bed feels comfortable.

D. The room or sheets smell good.
E. You have something to eat or drink before you retire.

18. When you are especially happy, everything:
A. Looks brighter.
B. Sounds clearer.
C. Feels comfortable or exciting.
D. Smells good.
E. Tastes better.

19. When arriving at the beach you first notice:
A. The look of the sand, sun, and waves.
B. The sound of the surf, wind and birds.
C. The feel of the sand and the heaviness of the air.
D. The smell of the ocean.
E. The taste of salt in the air.

20. When you go to a restaurant for the first time, what makes the strongest impression on you?
A. How the room is decorated and the dominant colors employed.
B. If it was loud or quiet as you ate.
C. How you felt, as in comfortable, cold, etc.
D. The way it smelled when you first walked in.
E. The taste of the food.

21. If you are suddenly frightened do you *first*:
A. Close your eyes.
B. Cover your ears.
C. Fold your arms and hold yourself tightly.
D. Breathe deeply through your nose.

E. Clamp down your teeth.

22. When you arise in the morning, you are happiest when:
A. The sun is shining or when it is raining.
B. The wind is blowing or you hear rain on the window.
C. You feel the warmth of being under the covers.
D. You smell the freshness of the morning air.
E. You first taste your morning coffee or tea.

23. At a party, your perspective changes when:
A. The lighting changes.
B. The music stops or changes volume or tempo.
C. The room becomes warmer or cooler.
D. You encounter someone with strong perfume or cologne.
E. You eat or drink something.

24. When eating an orange, what you remember most is:
A. The color of the skin and fruit.
B. The sound you make when you peel the skin or break apart the sections.
C. The feel of the fruit as you lift it to your mouth.
D. The smell of the orange.
E. The taste and texture as you eat it.

25. You know you are doing well at your job when:
A. You visualize yourself moving into a better office.
B. You hear a superior complementing you on your work.

C. You complete a particularly challenging project and get a feeling of satisfaction and relief.
D. You can smell success.
E. When a superior takes you to lunch or for a drink.

26. You get along best with people who:
A. See things the way you do.
B. Enjoy the same music as you.
C. Feel the same way that you do in most situations.
D. Smell pleasant to you.
E. Enjoy the same foods as you.

27. When you are strongly motivated the first effect is that:
A. You see things differently.
B. You begin to tell yourself about the advantages that lie ahead.
C. You feel physically excited.
D. You notice that scents are suddenly stronger.
E. You want to eat or drink something in celebration.

28. Which best describes death:
A. Blackness or entirely new sights.
B. Silence or entirely new sounds.
C. Lack of feeling or entirely new feelings.
D. The smell of rotting flesh.
E. Never eating again or always eating what you like best.

29. When someone first tells you they love you, you:
A. Take a mental snapshot of the moment.

B. Record the dialog in your head.
C. Feel warm and fuzzy all over.
D. Become very aware of the scents around you.
E. Find that your mouth is dry.

30. At the gym, you gain immediate satisfaction from:
A. Looking at yourself in the mirror as you exercise, or seeing your body take the shape you want.
B. Hearing the sounds of the machines as you use them, or compliments on how you look.
C. Feeling your muscles tone up and become firmer.
D. The smell of sweat as you work out.
E. The taste of cool water as you drink after a good workout.

31. You feel very secure when:
A. You see your mate and they are calm and happy.
B. You hear familiar soothing sounds.
C. You are in the arms of your mate.
D. You smell a familiar scent, such as cookies baking.
E. You are eating your favorite food or drink.

32. When working with numbers you:
A. Write them down.
B. Say them to yourself.
C. Use your fingers to count.
D. Need to breathe fresh air to concentrate.
E. Need to eat or drink to concentrate.

33. In high school the period that you liked best from the following list was:
A. Art.
B. Music or language.
C. Shop or sports.
D. Home Economics.
E. Lunch.

34. Which of the following statements would you most likely or most often make:
A. "Looks good to me."
B. "Sounds fine."
C. "Something doesn't feel right."
D. "The whole thing stinks."
E. "She is so sweet."

When you have completed all of the answers above, total the number of A's, B's, C's, D's and E's. The letter with the highest total will indicate your dominant representational system.

**A's=Visual B's=Auditory C's=Kinesthetic
D's=Olfactory E's=Gustatory**

Now that you understand what your dominant representational system is, begin to study others and determine *their* dominate representational systems. Continue to practice until you find this effortless and automatic. In the chapters that follow we will delve deeper into the identification of representational systems and types and how you can use this information to your advantage in your rapport and skills of persuasion.

4
Submodalities

Our representational systems can be further defined by their qualities and attributes, which are known as their submodalities. These are the components that compose the structure of the programmed information. Each representational system has its own specific submodalities corresponding to the sense that that system represents. Submodalities can best be expressed as the details of the stored information that combine to create our complete perception of any particular information.

By understanding the submodalities of the representational system used when a particular input was received and stored, we can better understand the way we, and others, communicate with the world. This provides us with yet another tool necessary to properly communicate with ourselves and with others. Think of it as understanding several languages, with the representational systems being the nouns and verbs of the language and the submodalities being the adjectives and adverbs used to further clarify and define the meaning of the input. Thus, when you encounter a situation or person that requires the use of a particular language, you have the ability to speak and understand any language that is used, and express anything you need to effectively in that language.

Fig. 3 illustrates the primary submodalities of each of the five sensory representational systems:

Representational System	Submodalities
Visual	Brightness, Color, Shape, Size, Spatial Location, Dimensionality, Focus, Clarity, Graininess, Distance, Contrast, Motion etc.
Auditory	Volume, Tone, Timbre, Pitch, Tempo, Rhythm, Duration, Location, Mono, Stereo, Clear, etc.
Kinesthetic	Temperature, Intensity, Size, Location, Duration, Texture, Pressure, Sharp or Dull, Weight, etc.
Olfactory	Sweetness, Pungency, Musky, etc.
Gustatory	Sweet, Sour, Salty, Bitter, Acid, etc.

Fig. 3: Representational System's Primary Submodalities

5
Sensory Acuity

Sensory acuity is our ability to detect fine distinctions in the input we receive, in terms of representational systems and their submodalities. Acuity can be exhibited in each (or all) of our representational systems. Those among us who can hear if an instrument is minutely out of tune or can determine exactly what note is being played just by hearing it are displaying their audio acuity. Visual acuity can be observed in those who can see the subtle differences in color and shading in a painting or sunset. Being able to feel the differences in the thickness of playing cards, or noticing a slight change in temperature is an example of kinesthetic acuity. A good sommelier tastes even the slightest variations between bottles of the same wine using his gustatory acuity. Some individuals are able to smell something burning long before others in the same room, due to their olfactory acuity. Observe the animal kingdom. Most animals have exceptional sensory acuity. We have all heard that an animal can "smell" if you fear them. Actually, we do not specifically give an "odor" of fear, but rather, the animal is reading the subtle, non-verbal cues that we send indicating the fear that we feel, and generally, their reaction to their observation of our fear is to become afraid themselves (mirror) and respond accordingly (match).

Our subconscious mind perceives every detail of every input of every representational system and their submodalities at all times. Individuals who exhibit acuity in a particular representational system have programmed their subconscious mind to respond to the input from that system by making their conscious mind become aware of all of the details of that input. Therefore, their subconscious mind notifies the conscious mind that the sound that was just heard was a B flat, or that the eye has just seen fifteen different shades of red in the painting they are viewing.

As a person passes from one state to another, they send out subtle verbal and non-verbal signals. The first step in effectively influencing the client is to accurately read their verbal and non-verbal cues and properly identify their dominant representational system. To do this we must program our subconscious mind to report the details of those signals, enabling us to appropriately respond to them.

The following sensory acuity exercises will help heighten your conscious awareness of your senses and sharpen your sensory acuity in all of them. In these exercises, we use self-hypnosis to gain access to our subconscious mind and then, because of the hyperacuity of the hypnotic state, we bring that ability back with us to our conscious state. Effectively, we begin to experience our senses in the same way that our subconscious mind always realizes them. To perform this exercise, you'll need to use the systems outlined in the appendices included at the back of this book.

<u>Visual acuity exercise</u>

1. Have a colorful painting or photograph available.
2. Relaxation exercise (Appendix A).

3. Induction of hypnosis (Appendix A).
4. Deepening (Appendix A).
5. Open your eyes and stare at the painting or photograph. While you are in the hypnotic state look at every detail. Stare at it for a very long time until you notice things that you did not notice before, such as variations in color, shadow and hue. Stare at it even longer until you can no longer find anything new.
6. Emergence (Appendix A).
7. Repeat step 5 while out of the hypnotic state and see if you can still find the same things you discovered while in the hypnotic state.

Audio acuity exercise

1. Have music playing, preferably a CD or a tape that can be set to repeat.
2. Relaxation exercise (Appendix A).
3. Induction of hypnosis (Appendix A).
4. Deepening (Appendix A).
5. With your eyes closed, listen to the music. Allow your ears to notice and hear every nuance of the music while in the hypnotic state. Isolate and listen to each instrument individually, separate from the others. Then combine them all together and find new and different sounds. Continue to listen until you notice things that you did not notice before, such as variations in pitch, tone or volume. Listen even longer until you can no longer find anything new.
6. Emergence (Appendix A).

7. Repeat step 5 while out of the hypnotic state and see if you can still find the same things you discovered while in the hypnotic state.

Kinesthetic acuity exercise

1. Have an item available that you can hold in your hand.
2. Relaxation exercise (Appendix A).
3. Induction of hypnosis (Appendix A).
4. Deepening (Appendix A).
5. With your eyes closed, grasp the object. Allow your fingers to notice and feel the texture, hardness and temperature of the object while in the hypnotic state. Hold it in different ways and spend time noticing everything you can about the object. Continue to touch and feel the object until you notice things that you did not notice before. Touch and handle the object for even longer until you can no longer find anything new.
6. Emergence (Appendix A).
7. Repeat step 5 while out of the hypnotic state and see if you can still find the same things you discovered while in the hypnotic state.

Gustatory acuity exercise

1. Have something you can taste available, such as a piece of fruit or glass of juice.
2. Relaxation exercise (Appendix A).
3. Induction of hypnosis (Appendix A).
4. Deepening (Appendix A).
5. With your eyes closed, put the food in your mouth. Allow your tongue to notice everything about the

flavor. Taste it in ways you never have before. Isolate every part of the flavor, the sweetness, the tartness, the intensity, and then isolate any sub-flavors you can find. Combine all of the flavors back together again. Continue to taste until you notice things that you did not notice before. Taste for even longer until you can no longer find anything new.
6. Emergence (Appendix A).
7. Repeat step 5 while out of the hypnotic state and see if you can still find the same things you discovered while in the hypnotic state.

<u>Olfactory acuity exercise</u>

1. Have a bottle of perfume, a flower or some other fragrant item available.
2. Relaxation exercise (Appendix A).
3. Induction of hypnosis (Appendix A).
4. Deepening (Appendix A).
5. With your eyes closed, smell the fragrance. Allow your nose to notice and smell every nuance of the fragrance while in the hypnotic state. Isolate and smell each distinct part of the fragrance, and any contributing fragrances, then combine them back together and find new and different characteristics of the aroma. Continue to smell the fragrance and notice things you did not notice before. Smell the fragrance even longer until you can no longer find anything new.
6. Emergence (Appendix A).
7. Repeat step 5 while out of the hypnotic state and see if you can still find the same things you discovered while in the hypnotic state.

These exercises should be repeated often using different items. At first you may notice only a few new characteristics. However, soon you will find unlimited variations. You will discover that after a few times, you will begin to see, hear, taste, feel and smell things in different and more detailed ways each time, even when you are not in a hypnotic state.

As we become proficient at reading the cues and learn the proper responses, these can also be programmed into our subconscious mind until eventually we can read and respond to a person's verbal and non verbal cues automatically, from a subconscious level, with no conscious involvement at all. Thus, we are able to identify their dominant representational system instantly and respond in kind during our interaction with them. This is a primary element of building rapport, as we will learn later.

6
Mind Aesthetics®

As we discuss Mind Aesthetics®, we must concern ourselves with the subconscious mind. The conscious mind is involved to such a lesser degree that it is nearly insignificant, so we will focus only on the subconscious mind in our discussion here, concentrating particularly on its power to control all of the muscles (voluntary and involuntary) in our body, and its unique tendency to accept suggestion and consequently be influenced and persuaded.

Since our subconscious mind *does* control all of the involuntary muscles in our body, it uses this power to express the way we feel inside - our deepest inner feelings -to the outside world by altering and modifying our muscles to display the way we truly feel. In this manner, our subconscious mind controls the way we appear to others, our posture and stance, our mannerisms, our pace, our voice, and, most significantly in light of our discussion here, our subconscious mind uses our face to display our feelings, altering and adjusting the muscles to show the world how we feel inside. If we feel anything less than beautiful inside, others can see this instantly simply by observing us, and particularly our face, as our subconscious mind has sculpted it, reflecting our deepest feelings at any given moment. Thus, in order for a client to *look* beautiful, they must first *feel* beautiful, on a subconscious level, deep inside,.

Those of us engaged in the field of beauty employ great efforts to correct and improve the way our clients appear, and while it is true that a facial will make their face feel fresh and revitalized, that a mask will smooth out the skin, that make-up will certainly enhance their external, physical appearance, and that a massage will soothe the muscles, all of these things do little or nothing to address the way they *feel* deep inside, and it is there that true beauty originates.

> *Aesthetics involve the mind as well as the body, and Mind Aesthetics® are more important to physical appearance then all the make-up, body wraps, and spa visits in the world!*
>
> *The mind is the most neglected part of any beauty regimen and, ironically, it is the most important.*

Additionally, we must remember that when a client feels beautiful on the inside they will express that wonderful feeling in many ways:

1. Repeat Business - by coming back frequently.
2. Referrals - by telling others about you.
3. Requesting You - and *only* you when they do return to the salon or spa.

And we all know that when a client feels especially good about and satisfied by the service we have provided, they will let us know by giving us a bigger tip! In other words, if the client feels beautiful inside when we complete their service *we* will realize the benefits on many, many levels.

To further illustrate this concept, consider the frown. We have all heard that it takes more muscles to frown than to smile. In fact, this is true. More work, effort and energy are necessary to produce a frown than a smile. A frown is a deliberate expression. No less then seventy-two muscles in the face must be activated in a specific configuration for a frown to appear, as opposed to only fourteen for a smile, and yet, if we look around us at people we encounter on the street, in the mall and in our place of business, we notice immediately that most of them are frowning! And why is that? They have not all just received some devastating or depressing news. They cannot all be currently involved in some catastrophic life crisis. No, the reason that most of them are frowning is because they do not *feel* good, deep inside, on a subconscious level. They do not feel beautiful, and their subconscious mind, which controls all of the involuntary muscles in their bodies, manifests that feeling, expressing it and displaying it to the outside world, using their faces as canvases on which their true feelings are painted.

Therefore, in order to apply aesthetics to the client's mind, we must guide him or her toward positive thoughts of well-being. We persuade and influence the client, preparing their subconscious to accept our suggestions, then literally telling them how they should feel. This is our desired outcome, our goal. A successful visit to any salon or spa results in the client feeling better *inside* as well as out when they leave than they did when they arrived. If we only concern ourselves with the external we are not truly servicing the client properly. Mind Aesthetics® is also a tremendous way to build client loyalty, and consequently repeat business and referrals, all adding up to an increase in our bottom line.

When a client leaves our salon or spa feeling beautiful inside we have done them a great service, and subconsciously they realize that we were responsible for the positive improvement in their state. Their subconscious mind will give us the credit! Imagine the value of your clients thinking to themselves, "Every time I come here and you take care of me I always leave feeling wonderful no matter how I felt when I arrived! This is a great place! I must come back here ... often!"

Remember, it is human nature that spurs us to move toward pleasure and that which our subconscious mind has recorded as positively improving our physical and mental state, and away from that which does not.

As humans we prefer to feel good, we like it, and we make every effort to regain that feeling whenever it is lost. Albeit misguided, this becomes the other driving force in the quest for beauty that I referred to earlier (***Beauty***). As we have learned through experience that when we feel good we look good, I believe that one of the primary forces that compels us to look beautiful is the need to feel good again when that feeling has been lost, our need to feel beautiful once more. That is, we believe that if we improve our external appearance, it will change the way we feel inside, at the subconscious level. Although there is some merit to the notion that improving the way we look externally makes us feel better, in fact, this concept is flawed. It simply does not work both ways. In order to look good, we must feel good, but looking good alone is not sufficient to change the way we feel inside.

Therefore we can summarize our quest for beauty as follows: 1) The instinctual tendency toward the natural selection of the fittest mate, and our desire to be chosen as such, to be accepted, and 2) Our desire to feel good deep inside, on the subconscious level, and our mistaken reasoning that improving our external appearance will achieve that goal.

The fact that our logic may be flawed in no way diminishes the need to satisfy that drive within us. A desire is a desire, even if we feel it for the wrong reasons, and we are compelled to fulfill our desires. Consequently, when we make someone feel beautiful inside, we are satisfying two very important and basic needs that exist within them. The commercialization of beauty merely exploits these needs to sell more products and services, frequently with little or no benefit to the client and even less concern for the way they truly feel. Mind Aesthetics®, by contrast, *addresses* these needs directly and fulfills them. A happy by-product of the Mind Aesthetics® process is that we benefit *along with* the client, rather than at their expense.

More important, however, is the fact that by making someone feel beautiful inside, we are genuinely improving their physical and mental state, their life. This is the greatest value of Mind Aesthetics®.

We can summarize the primary two goals of Mind Aesthetics® as follows:

> 1) Reaching the client's subconscious mind during normal interaction and conversation by utilizing and carefully implementing techniques which create an environment wherein we develop a strong, indelible bond with them, causing them to become responsive and receptive to our suggestions, giving us an enormous advantage in our ability to influence and persuade them to purchase products and services as well as maintain them as frequent, repeat clients whose satisfaction and contentment compel them to refer others to us.
>
> 2) With access to the client's subconscious mind established, instilling within them an

overwhelmingly positive energy, a feeling of comfort and peace that causes them to feel beautiful inside and out, resulting in dramatically improving their physical and mental state, while actually enhancing their external physical appearance and bringing them to levels of relaxation that many of them have never experienced in their lives.

To accomplish these two goals, Mind Aesthetics® provides two methods:

1) The application of the Mind Aesthetics® Techniques which are explained in this book. You will learn the techniques and how to properly utilize them when interacting with your client to rapidly enter rapport with them and prepare them to accept the carefully worded suggestions you will be taught how to give. These interactive techniques can be used to implant suggestions of a persuasive and influential nature as well as suggestions designed to improve your services by improving the way your clients perceive and experience them while enhancing the client's physical and emotional state, making them feel beautiful inside as well as out.

2.) The Mind Aesthetics® CD which automatically lulls your client into a deep state of relaxation and suggestibility, with or without your active participation, and then applies a "treatment" directly to their subconscious mind, replacing negative ideas with positive energy and the feeling of well-being from the inside. This revolutionary new approach to the field of beauty is designed to cause your clients to become and remain loyal, repeat clients, increase the number of referrals you receive and consequently improve your bottom line. The Mind Aesthetics® CD automates the process of preparing the client to receive your suggestions of persuasion and enhancement, leaves them feeling wonderful and beautiful inside and out and presents still another opportunity for you to offer effective suggestions with the client in the proper state to accept and follow them. The results of using The Mind Aesthetics® CD have been incredible. A detailed explanation of The Mind Aesthetics® CD can be found later in this book.

7
Zone Exercise

The first step in the application of Mind Aesthetics® requires us to examine ourselves, ensuring that no conflicts exist between our subconscious mind and our body. Remember, our subconscious mind expresses the way we feel inside to the outside world, so before we can "sell" the client on the idea of feeling beautiful inside, we must first feel this way ourselves. Doing so creates a force around us that others can sense, and feel, and even see ... a glow that emanates positive energy - and we all know that positive energy is very easy to pass on to others.

The need for self-preparation cannot be overstated. For example, if you were to bring your clothes to a tailor and *his* outfit did not fit him properly, it would have a direct effect on your decision to have him do your alterations. If you needed bodywork for your car and the shop owner drove a beat-up, dented wreck, you would take your business elsewhere. Who among us would consider the services of an overweight, out of shape personal trainer? Well, the same is true when applying Mind Aesthetics®, and there are reasons beyond those that apply to the previous examples. As you will see when we discuss rapport, the Mind Aesthetics® application creates a bond between you and your client, resulting in a mutual exchange, a sharing of emotional energy. If your energy is negative, it will have the effect of worsening the client's state and alienating you from them, greatly hindering your ability to influence them. Additionally, by failing to properly prepare yourself, you may create a barrier - a wall - that tells the client, "stay away". Believe me, if you do that, they will avoid you at all costs!

We must, therefore, invest some time in preparing ourselves. This will benefit us as well as the client. Fortunately, as you practice self-preparation, you will find that it becomes easier and easier, until soon it is automatic, and you know what? You will feel better and be better for it!

Consider a successful, professional athlete. Before a game he or she will prepare themselves, adjusting their mental attitude and establishing perfect communication between their subconscious mind and their body. Many of them call this the *Zone*. The Zone is a state in which their subconscious mind and their body are in perfect synchronization, both on the same page. They *know* what they are about to do and they *feel* what they are about to do. This prepares them for the challenge they are about to face, and puts them in the mode of top performance. It puts them in full control, and enables them to play the very best they can, frequently better then ever before, as they harness the power of their subconscious mind and allow it to control their muscles and actions. Often, the best players will explain that when they play they are not consciously aware of what they are doing, they just allow their subconscious mind to take over and they perform better then they possibly could with conscious interference. When asked to describe the Zone, many will explain it as a state in which everyone around them is moving very slowly as they are moving quickly with increased sensory acuity and awareness. This

Zone Exercise

effect, know as *time distortion*, occurs when our subconscious mind takes control from our conscious mind. Martial Arts Masters utilize time distortion as a method of giving them added time to prepare their counter attacks as their opponent attacks in "slow motion".

Another reported characteristic of being in the Zone is the presence of extremely sharp and acute reflexes. This is the result of the heightened, sharpened state that our senses acquire when our subconscious mind is in control, like the case of the mother who is able, in a moment of crisis, to lift a two ton car that has fallen on her child. In such a circumstance, her subconscious mind has taken over and utilized its power over her muscles to accomplish what needed to be done without the limitations that conscious evaluation causes. Traumatic events that elicit fear and other powerful emotions frequently cause the conscious mind to be bypassed and the subconscious to take control. However, drastic and dramatic events are not the only times our subconscious can be activated. Consider a great concert pianist. Many of the greatest musicians allow their subconscious minds to control the movements of their hands, fingers and breathing, producing wonderful results. As a matter of fact, most good musicians will tell you that if they were to watch their hands as they play, or consciously think of the next note in the sequence, they would be unable to proceed and would begin to play incorrect notes. The best performances, in all fields, originate in, and are orchestrated by, the subconscious mind.

We must also enter the Zone, so to speak, before interacting with our clients, to ensure that we feel beautiful inside so the energy we emanate is all positive. We cannot ask someone else to experience something that we ourselves do not feel. Beyond that, the benefits you personally will gain from feeling beautiful inside provide more then sufficient reason to enter the Zone and prepare yourself properly.

The exercise outlined below in great detail will assist you in entering the Zone and preparing yourself before you see your clients. Read through it completely before you practice it.

Entering The Zone

1. Find a Quiet Place - Especially when you first employ this exercise it is important that you find a place where you can concentrate without interruption. This allow you to focus all of your energy and attention properly to achieve the maximum benefit. As with any art or skill, eventually you will find that you can enter the Zone spontaneously in any environment. It may take only one or it may take several practices of the exercise to feel the full effect.

2. Breath Deeply - Stand in an uncluttered spot with sufficient space all around you. Take at least three deep breaths, holding them for thirty or forty seconds before releasing them. As you release your breaths, allow yourself to relax, dropping your shoulders as you exhale. Focus on your breathing to the exclusion of everything around you. Turn all of your attention inward, hearing and feeling your heartbeat and becoming very aware of your inner self. Notice how easily you are able to shut out the outside, and contact your inner core of energy as your breathing causes you to become more relaxed and focused.

3. Identify the State You Wish To Enter - As you continue to relax and breathe deeply, begin to go back in your mind and time, back to an event or occasion

Zone Exercise

when you felt the heightened state you are seeking to reproduce. A time when everything was going right, when you were in complete control. It can be anywhere, anytime. It may be a work-related experience, or recreational, or when you were in school, at home or with friends. The location and time of the experience is not important but rather the feeling you had when it occurred. That feeling that you were in control. Everything you did went exactly the way you wanted. You knew exactly what you wanted to do, and how, and it went exactly that way for you. You were "Wonder Woman" or "Superman" that day, and everything you touched seemed to go perfectly. If you were with clients that day, each service went just as it should. A feeling of contentment and satisfaction was within you as you achieved precisely what you intended to and, above all, you were able to reach your goal effortlessly. In all, the experience represents how you would like things to be every single day. If you have never had such an experience, as unlikely as this is, try visualizing someone you know who has, and imagine how their experience felt. "Become" them and feel what they felt. Once you acquire this image or feeling, hold on to it.

4. Visualize Or Imagine Your Circle - From where you are standing, picture a circle large enough for you to stand in on the floor in front of you. Inside that circle imagine all of the characteristics of that wonderful experience when things were perfect. This circle is *your* circle. It contains every aspect of the experience, all that you recall and even facets that you may have forgotten. Your circle is filled with all of the positive energy of that experience, and all of the power that accompanied it. Look deeply into your circle until you begin to see and feel the energy within it. Notice the dominant color that shows itself as a haze or glow within your circle. Become aware of any and all of the characteristics that reveal themselves within your circle.

5. Close Your Eyes And Enter Your Circle - Now that the state has been identified and your circle contains all of the characteristics and energy of that state, close your eyes, and *keep them closed for the remainder of the exercise.* Take a step forward into your circle and notice the surge of energy that immediately enters your body and flows to every corner of it. Allow the energy to move through you without restriction, flowing from head to toe, through every nerve and capillary. Enjoy the jolt of energy as it fills your being, and notice how good it feels to accept its flow, its strength, its power. As you stand in your circle, lose any remaining contact with the outside world and become one with the energy as it overwhelms you.

6. Recall Entirely The Experience When You Were In The State - As you stand in your circle, filled with the energy of that time in your past when everything was perfect, recall entirely the experience of that state. Relive the memory. Enter it, and allow it to re-enter you, flowing through every bone, muscle and fiber of your being. With each of your senses relive all of the characteristics of the experience, every nuance of the state. Become one, once again, with the feeling. Become the state. Gradually bring your focus to each of your senses, one by one, and re-experience that wonderful state exactly as you did when it first

Zone Exercise

occurred. Explore each of your senses one by one, as the energy of the state grows stronger and stronger with each passing second.

<u>Visual:</u> Bring your focus and all of your attention to your sense of sight and become aware of all aspects of your sense of sight. Allow the energy of the state to grow stronger. Look around you, while keeping your eyes closed.

> What do you see?
> Is your vision wide or narrow?
> Are the colors sharp and clear?
> What is the dominant color you see as you experience the state?
> Become very aware of the dominant color and notice how often it appears.
> Are things moving or are they still?
> If they are moving, describe their speed.
> Do you see others around you? What are they doing?
> Look around you (while keeping your eyes closed) and describe the scene.
> What other aspects do you notice involving your sight?

Experience fully all aspects of your visual sense and allow it to grow and intensify, becoming stronger and more detailed.

<u>Auditory:</u> Now bring your focus and all of your attention to your auditory sense, your sense of hearing. Allow the energy of the state to grow stronger. Listen around you.

What do you hear?
Are the sounds muffled or clear?
Are they loud or soft?
Are they all around you, or coming from one direction?
Are they close or in the distance?
Describe the particular sounds you hear.
Identify the sound that is most pronounced, the dominant sound.
Become very aware of the dominant sound and notice the energy you receive from it.
Are other sounds contributing to the energy and power of the state?
What exactly is your internal dialog, the voice within you, saying?
What other aspects do you notice involving your sense of hearing?

Experience fully all aspects of your auditory sense and allow it to grow and intensify, becoming stronger and more detailed.

<u>Kinesthetic:</u> Now bring your focus and all of your attention to your kinesthetic sense, your sense of feel and touch. Allow the energy of the state to grow stronger. Feel everything around you.

What do you feel?
Do you feel light or heavy?
Where would you describe your center to be?
Describe how you feel inside, physically.

Zone Exercise

> Are you grounded firmly to the earth, or light and floating?
> Are you calm yet energized?
> Is the air around you dry or moist?
> Do you feel warm or cool?
> Identify the dominant feeling, the one you notice most or feel the strongest.
> Become very aware of this dominant feeling and notice the energy you receive from it.
> What other aspects involving your sense of feel and touch do you notice?

Experience fully all aspects of your kinesthetic sense and allow it to grow and intensify, becoming stronger and more detailed.

<u>Olfactory:</u> Now bring your focus and all of your attention to your olfactory sense, your sense of smell. Allow the energy of the state to grow stronger. Breathe around you.

> Describe the fragrances around you.
> Are they strong or subtle?
> Are they pleasant?
> Identify the dominant fragrance or odor.
> Become very aware of the dominant fragrance and notice the energy you receive from it.
> What other aspects involving your sense of smell do you notice?

Make-Up Their Mind

Experience fully all aspects of your olfactory sense and allow it to grow and intensify, becoming stronger and more detailed.

Gustatory: Now bring your focus and all of your attention to your gustatory sense, your sense of taste. Allow the energy of the state to grow stronger. Explore the tastes.

> Describe the tastes in your mouth.
> Are they strong or subtle?
> Are they pleasant?
> Identify the dominant taste.
> Become very aware of the dominant taste and notice the energy you receive from it.
> What other aspects involving your sense of taste do you notice?

Experience fully all aspects of your gustatory sense and allow it to grow and intensify, becoming stronger and more detailed.

Other Sensations: Now bring your focus and all of your attention to any other characteristics of this state that present themselves to you. Allow the energy of the state to grow stronger. Experience them fully.

> Describe fully any other aspects of the state that you are aware of.
> Identify the dominant characteristics of each aspect.
> Become very aware of the dominant characteristics and notice the energy you receive from them.

Zone Exercise

Experience fully all aspects of these other sensations and allow them to grow and intensify, becoming stronger and more detailed.

Spend another moment to relive entirely everything you have just identified. Enjoy the energy. Become one with the entire state, and allow it to spread and grow, becoming stronger and stronger with each breath you take, each beat of your heart. When you are truly one with the experience, and reliving it completely, continue to step 7.

7. Exit Your Circle And Break The State - Now take one step back out of the circle, and break the state while keeping your eyes closed. Take a deep breath and hold it for thirty to forty seconds before releasing it. Shake off the energy from the circle and neutralize yourself. Take a moment to return to a normal, neutral state. Recall a time when you were not in the state, perhaps when you were stuck in traffic, at a boring lecture or class, or at work when things were just normal. When you have returned to normal on every level, proceed to step 8.

8. Re-enter Your Circle And Relive The Experience Again - Now re-enter your circle while keeping your eyes closed and notice how quickly and completely it re-elicits the state, how just entering causes you to immediately re-experience that wonderful feeling. Notice how it returns even stronger and stronger, with more energy then the last time you entered your circle. Become very aware of each of your senses and how they have returned with a jolt to the feelings you described when last in your circle. Quickly run through each of your senses and each of the characteristics you mentioned earlier.

Visual: Once again bring your focus and all of your attention to your sense of sight and recall all aspects of your sense of sight. Allow the energy of the state to grow stronger. Notice each of the aspects of the state as you recalled them before, listing each characteristic and noticing how re-entering your circle has caused them to become even stronger. Recall the dominant color, the motion, etc. Notice also that you are able to recall aspects that you had forgotten as the experience becomes more and more intense, more and more real.

Experience fully all aspects of your visual sense and allow them to grow and intensify, becoming stronger and stronger, more and more detailed.

Auditory: Again bring your focus and all of your attention to your auditory sense, your sense of hearing. Allow the energy of the state to grow stronger. Notice each aspect of the state as you recalled it before and list each characteristic of your sense of hearing. Notice how re-entering the circle has caused these characteristics to intensify as well. Become aware of additional sound-related characteristics that you missed last time and allow them to join the energy of the experience.

Experience fully all aspects of your auditory sense and allow them to grow and intensify, becoming stronger and stronger, more and more detailed.

Kinesthetic: Now bring your focus and all of your attention to your kinesthetic sense, your sense of feel and touch. Allow the energy of the state to grow stronger. Relive each aspect of this sense and list each characteristic as you recalled them when last in your circle. Notice how they have intensified, how being in your circle has caused them to grow and become more clear to you. Become aware of additional kinesthetic characteristics that you did not feel earlier and experience them completely. Become one with the energy of the feeling as it grows and intensifies, becoming stronger and more detailed.

Olfactory: Now, once again, bring your focus and all of your attention to your olfactory sense, your sense of smell. Allow the energy of the state to grow stronger. Notice how being in your circle causes their immediate return. Relive and recall fully the dominant fragrance and notice how you are now able to recall other scents that eluded you earlier. Experience them fully and allow them to grow and intensify, becoming stronger and stronger, more and more detailed.

Gustatory: One more time, bring your focus and all of your attention to your gustatory sense, your sense of taste. Allow the energy of the state to grow stronger. Become very aware of the dominant taste and notice the energy you receive from it and how being in your circle causes it to return instantly. Allow this experience to grow and intensify, becoming stronger and stronger, more and more detailed.

Other Sensations: Finally, include any other characteristics of this state that present themselves to you. Allow the energy of the state to grow stronger. Experience them fully, and notice the new ones. Become very aware of the dominant characteristics and notice the energy you receive from them.

Experience fully all aspects of these other sensations and allow them to grow and intensify, becoming stronger and stronger, more and more detailed.

Take another moment and notice how being in your circle causes the entire experience to return fully and completely, with every nuance, and how very wonderful it feels.

9. Exit Your Circle And Break The State - Now take one step back out of the circle, and break the state while keeping your eyes closed. Take a deep breath and hold it for thirty to forty seconds before releasing it. Shake off the energy from the circle and neutralize yourself. Take a moment to return to a normal, neutral state, again recalling a time when you were not in the state. When you have returned to normal on every level, proceed to step 10.

10. Re-enter Your Circle And Relive The Experience - Re-enter your circle (while keeping your eyes closed) and notice how the totality of the state returns instantly - with the speed and intensity of a bolt of lightning entering your body, moving through your being, to each and every corner, every cell, every nerve, every fiber. You feel uplifted and full of the wonderful energy and you can instantly recall, with all of your senses, every single detail of the experience. It grows, stronger and stronger and stronger, reaching a peak, an apex. It is becoming stronger than ever before, even stronger than when you first experienced it, and it feels wonderful.

Allow the feeling to reach its peak, its strongest point, and then let it get even stronger. When it is deeply

Zone Exercise

intense, stronger, and more powerful and you are one with it, proceed to step 11.

11. Set Your Anchor - When that feeling is at its strongest point, at its peak, its apex, and you are feeling its wholly positive energy with your entire being, make an OK sign with the thumb and index finger of one hand. As you make that OK sign, notice how the touch of your thumb to your index finger triggers another jolt, as it assumes the same power of your circle, the power to elicit this feeling instantly. Make that OK sign and feel the power, the energy, the intensity. As the feeling is at its peak make that OK sign and hold it, allowing it to elicit the feeling.

12. Exit Your Circle And Break The State - Once again, exit your circle and release the OK sign as you do, still with closed eyes. Break the state and shake off the feeling, neutralizing yourself once more. Calm yourself and remove yourself from the feeling, becoming once again totally normal and neutral.

13. Test Your Anchor - Now, while standing outside your circle, with your eyes closed, and in a neutral state, make the OK sign and notice how it causes every detail of the state, every characteristic and nuance, to return to you instantly, preparing you, putting you in the Zone, all with the touch of your finger. Making the OK sign now elicits that wonderful feeling and prepares you exactly as entering your circle did earlier. Feel that rush of energy, that jolt, as you make the OK sign and the feeling spreads like lightning through your entire being. Open your eyes now, and notice that the feeling remains, and will remain for as long as you like, even after you release the OK sign.

This exercise may be used as frequently as desired or necessary until the anchor functions exactly the way you want it to. Eventually the anchor will become permanent and the exercise will no longer be required to enter the state. For some, this will occur after only one use of the exercise, for others it may take several. Continue to use the exercise until the anchor triggers the state spontaneously upon firing it. It will also become quickly apparent to you that each time you fire the anchor and trigger the state, it will return quicker, stronger and more easily.

It is important to note also that anything can be used as the anchor for this exercise. It can be anchored visually to something you look at when you want to enter the state, or to a sound or a fragrance. Even a thought can be used as an anchor to trigger the state.

With this exercise we are properly prepared, we feel beautiful inside. Now that we are in the state we need to be in, we can begin our interaction with our clients. This preparation, our self-preparation, is crucial to the process of influencing the client and reaching our intended goal of making them feel beautiful inside. Without proper preparation, we would be unable to bring them to the state they need to enter. Remember, our interaction as well as our ability to influence our clients involves sharing to a large degree, and we cannot share that which we do not have within us. If we have any negativity within us, that too is shared with the client, achieving exactly the opposite of our intention. We have all had the experience of being brought down from a positive state by someone who did not share our energy. It is not pleasant. I cannot overstate the significance and importance of proper self-preparation before the implementation of any Mind Aesthetics®

Zone Exercise

techniques. For this reason, I have dedicated so many pages to detailing the steps to proper self-preparation and entering the Zone. Be certain to consider it with the weight and importance that it requires to ensure your success in the strategies that follow.

8
Rapport

Once prepared, we are in the state we need to be in to emanate the energy to properly interact with, influence and guide the client and reach our ultimate goal of making them feel beautiful inside.

The first step in client interaction is to establish *rapport*. The word "rapport" is French, literally meaning, "to bring or offer back", (you will see the how appropriate that becomes when we discuss Mirroring and Matching). The French use the word most often in the expression, "en rapport avec", which can be translated as "to be in connection with someone." For our purposes we explain rapport as meaning the quality of trust, agreement and cooperation resulting in a reciprocal acceptance that occurs between individuals, enabling them to relate to and communicate perfectly with each other. We might further define rapport as a state of harmony and recognition between people, an acceptance and mutual understanding that results in a sense of ease and comfort. Congruency. It occurs naturally when people are in "sync" or in "tune" with each other, such as when they share common interests. However, rapport does

Make-Up Their Mind

not always occur spontaneously or naturally. When it does not exist naturally, it can be developed by one person entering the other's reality and communicating with them on their level.

In understanding rapport it is important to realize that each person builds their own unique map of the world. Everything they do, feel, think or experience, every decision they ever make, every conclusion they ever draw is based entirely on their map, rather than the world itself. Their map becomes their perspective of the world, and everything they perceive and understand is based on *and skewed by* their perception of the world. This becomes their reality. Rapport can exist only where a sharing of that reality is present between individuals. Thus we must identify the client's reality, understand it, and enter it.

Everyone has been in rapport at one time or another. We have all had the experience of interacting with someone and leaving them feeling good and very positive. Losing all track of the time while we were together. Becoming so absorbed and immersed in the moment and the conversation that we may even forget for a moment where we are. Then, when we part, we leave with the feeling that the person is really special, perhaps even thinking "what a great person," and feeling that we were pretty special too. That is rapport. When you are talking with someone, a spouse, a co-worker, a friend, and you are in rapport, you may open your mouth to speak at the same moment, maybe even to say exactly the same thing. This is rapport too. Rapport is an essential element of all effective communication.

Perhaps you have had the experience of meeting someone for the first time and feeling quite disinterested in them, but after having spent a short time conversing with them, finding your barriers broken down. You suddenly feel very close to them and cannot even recall why you avoided that closeness at first. Maybe you even feel a little guilty for

Rapport

your previously somewhat rude behavior. If so, you have just experienced how rapidly rapport can be built by a skilled practitioner.

Many successful waiters and waitresses are skilled in the art of rapport-building. Think back to a time when you went to a restaurant and, at first, were somewhat unimpressed. Perhaps the decor was not to your liking or some other factor just interfered with your enjoyment of the experience. Then you were made to wait longer then you felt appropriate and you actually began to ask yourself why you were even there. You are finally seated and your server greets you. In a short time, his or her conversation and personality soothes you and soon you begin to feel more comfortable and start to enjoy yourself, feeling an affinity with the server. By the end of the meal you are having a great time and you comment on how wonderful the service was. You may even feel empathy for the server, whose excellent talents are being inhibited by his employers' policies and a staff of less competent co-workers. You have joined the servers "team". You are on his side. It's you and him against the "others". In fact, you did not even notice that the mashed potatoes were cold and the steak slightly overcooked.

People in love are in rapport. They share many things in common and generally have the same goals, morals, ideals and objectives.

Effective persuasive communication can only exist when rapport exists. Think, for a moment, about the last time you were very uncomfortable being around someone. Perhaps you were angry with them. If they spoke, you probably did not even hear or remember (or care) what they said. If they asked you to do something you immediately rejected the request without even considering it. Conversely, if you think about the last time you felt very comfortable and close to someone, you most probably hung on their every word, and would have done anything they asked. This is the magic of rapport.

As stated earlier, rapport can occur naturally and spontaneously between two people who share many similarities and discover them instinctively on meeting. More frequently, however, rapport must be built. There are many ways to rapidly, even instantly, develop rapport with your client, and we will examine the techniques and steps involved. Perhaps the greatest skill required in the art of developing, entering and building rapport with another is the ability to implement the rapport by building techniques smoothly and effortlessly so that they flow naturally rather then appearing to be scripted. Rapport cannot be effectively built if the client believes they are being manipulated or you are doing something "to" them. Thus, incorporating rapport-building skills into your routine and practicing them until they are a function of your subconscious mind, implemented spontaneously and automatically, with no conscious thought involved, becomes the most effect method of utilizing them, and consequently our primary objective in learning the techniques.

Developing the skill of effective, rapid rapport-building also requires that you become very observant, aware of the client's verbal and, more importantly, their non-verbal communication (thus the importance of good sensory acuity skills). Less than ten percent of what we relay to each other is done through what we actually say. In fact, studies have shown that only about seven percent of what we communicate to each other is done through words. The qualities of our voice, that is, volume, speed, tone, etc. accounts for another thirty-eight percent of our communication. We all know it is not always *what* you say, but *how* you say it. For example, how many of us remember being punished when we were young for saying a perfectly acceptable word with the inflection of the curse word we were really thinking? And we all recall how we could immediately tell if we were in trouble, and even the degree of trouble we were in, just by the way our mother said one word: our name! She did not have to say anything else for us to get the message.

To illustrate this further, here is something you can try. Turn your TV to a foreign language show, one in a language that you do not understand at all, and watch the movie for a while. Even though you do not understand a single word being said, you will easily be able to follow the flow of the show, the attitude and emotions of all of the characters, simply by the way they speak. You may even be able to figure out the gist of the dialog by the inflections in their voices.

The other fifty-five or so percent, clearly the majority, of our communication with each other is transmitted through non-verbal communication, such as gestures, body language, expressions, eye movements, etc. Let us get back to mom for a moment. Remember how she could assume that certain stance, her body and arms in that particular position, her posture just so, and those eyes! Without saying a word you could look into those eyes and almost hear the rage as they "spoke" to you sternly saying, "You know what you did . . . and you know what's coming next!" All this without ever uttering a word!

We can see that non-verbal communication is even more important in rapport-building than what we say. When building rapport we must concentrate greatly on the client's and our own non-verbal language as well as our words.

These communicative qualities, which we observe as "cues", both verbal and more importantly non-verbal, are the factors that we use to identify representational systems and types, and to understand the language that the client is using to communicate. Only then can we enter the client's reality and influence their thinking and how they feel, and actually elicit specific responses from them, giving us a tremendous advantage in our ability to sell them products and services, and maintain them as loyal, repeat customers responsible for many referrals.

Establishing rapport becomes a simple process of reading the cues that are given by the client and then pacing, and mirroring and matching them to gain agreement, trust and congruency.

9
Reading The Client - Representational Types

We begin our reading of the client the moment we see them, even before either of us starts to speak. Observe the way they walk and stand, how they are dressed and in general how they appear. For example, if they are standing slumped forward with their shoulders dropped, head hanging and eyes drooping, they are likely to be depressed. An understanding of the client's demeanor helps us to better understand what and how they are thinking and enables us to enter their world and establish rapport more quickly.

From the first moment we see them we must begin to identify their dominant representational system. Below is a comprehensive listing of each of the three major representational systems, Visual, Auditory and Kinesthetic, and the common characteristics of a person whose dominant representational system corresponds to each. They are classified by Speech, Gestures, Head Position, Face Color,

Language, Eye Movement, Breathing, Dress, Thought Process, and other notable characteristics. Olfactory and Gustatory have been omitted as they are very unusual in our culture.

Remember that the dominant representational system is dynamic and may change from time to time, depending on the circumstances. Also, keep in mind that a person will frequently display characteristics from more than one of the representational systems, as we experience things from all of our senses all of the time. In this case, our objective is to determine which representational system the client is favoring at the current time, and we do so by determining which one has the majority of matches with the client's behavior. Some of the information in this chapter comes from the fine work of Dr. William Horton, an NLP colleague and friend, who has organized it quite succinctly.

Visual (sight)

Visuals are the majority, comprising sixty or more percent of the population. They base their reality on how things appear to them, how they see things. They are very aware of colors, shapes, brightness, etc. They think in images and thus process information very rapidly, being able to understand a complete story in one mental snapshot. The comedian Robin Williams is good example of a visual.

> Speech - Visuals are very quick to speak and generally do not demonstrate great deal of patience. They will speak very quickly, with their words and thoughts rapidly coming out in short bursts. Their sentences will often not end, speaking in "sound bites" giving you just enough information, creating a staccato

pattern of garbled words. Never attempt to interrupt a visual until they have completed their train of thought, as they will simply not permit you to enter the conversation until they do. To them, communication is done as quickly as possible and they process all input as images, usually in color.

Gestures - Just as a visual's speech is quick and jerky, their mannerisms are also, and they are generally quite animated and move about using their hands and body to emphasize their speech. They will "show" you what they are trying to tell you by using their body to demonstrate the point whenever possible. For example, if they tell you about an acrobat they recently saw, they will wave their arms and run and jump to make sure you understand the movements they are recalling visually. If they think you did not understand, of if they lose your attention, they will demonstrate again until they are satisfied that you understand. Their face is also very expressive and you can easily read their thoughts by observing their facial expressions.

When a visual is listening or observing, they may place their hand on their face with a finger pointing to their eye and they will rub their eyes often.

Head Position - Visuals will usually tilt their head up, in an effort to see everything around them clearly.

Face Color - Pale

Language - Visuals use sight-related expressions when they speak, such as:

"I see what you mean."
"Get the picture?"
"Looks ok to me."
"Can we focus on the subject?"
"Clearly you do not understand."
"I saw it coming."
"Don't shade the issue."
Refer to the list of predicates in the _Representational Systems_ chapter for additional words visuals would use.

Eye Movement - They will access memories as pictures, moving their eyes up and to the left for something remembered and up and to the right for something created.
Refer to the _Eye Accessing Cues_ chapter for additional details.

Breathing - The visual does nearly everything fast and their breathing will be shallow, in the upper part of the chest. When they talk, they often speak so quickly and furiously that they will become short of breath. They inhale in quick, short spurts.

Dress - Visuals conceptualize things as pictures and consequently are very driven by how things appear. Their dress will generally be very colorful, bright and well matched. They enjoy being ornate and will wear attractive jewelry

Reading The Client - Representational Types

and many accessories. In short, they are very careful about how they look. However, if they are in a crisis that involves personal matters that pre-occupy their minds, scattering their thoughts, it will be obvious as their dress will reflect the distraction, perhaps by being less colorful and more mis-matched. Under these circumstances they will tend to dress down.

Thought Process - Once again, visuals process all input as images, which is the fastest method of information processing. Their map of the world is displayed in pictures. Think of it as the speed of light (images) as opposed to, for example, the auditory who processes at the speed of sound. Consequently they think very, very quickly, often more quickly then they can express their thoughts, and will become easily frustrated if you are unable to keep up with them, or if they cannot make themselves clear to you immediately.

Other Characteristics - They need to be shown things, and require the information to be short, brief, to the point, and very visual. The information must also be precise. If a visual finds your information to be inaccurate, they will be hesitant to rely on you for information in the future. They become bored easily, since they process information so quickly, and must have a constant stream of new input. They are the movers and shakers of society, usually living in cities where there is lots of light and color to satisfy their visual needs. They are generally quite social and enjoy talking to many people at a party to keep from getting bored. Color and brightness are their friends. They function best in lighter colored rooms - a dull, dim room will slow them down and may even agitate them.

Auditory (sound)

Auditories are the second most common, comprising about twenty-five percent of the population. They base their reality on how things sound to them, how they hear things. They are very aware of tones, volume, silence, etc. They think in the way things sound and thus process information less rapidly then the visual, preferring to take information in as a story. Former President Ronald Reagan is a good example of an auditory.

Speech - Auditories usually speak slowly and rhythmically, with a musical quality to their speech. They prefer to be thorough in their speech to insure that they have said all the words necessary to relay their meaning accurately. They are conversational, however, and generally their conversation has a purpose. What others may consider small talk or excessive elaboration may be their way to receive more input or clarify the input that has already been received. They will generally expect some point to be made in a conversation. An auditory will choose his words carefully and frequently will end a sentence on an up inflection as if everything they say were phrased as a question. This is done to elicit a response from the listener, as we all generally respond spontaneously to the

Reading The Client - Representational Types

sound of a question. Unlike visuals, the auditory believes that words are the best way to express themselves and they will often be very detailed and colorful in their descriptions.

Gestures - An auditory can carry on an entire conversation without ever moving their hands. Words are their tool of communication. Their facial expressions are often fixed and unrevealing of the way they feel. If they are listening to something intently, they may place their hand on their face with a finger pointing to their ear. Auditories will touch their ears often. They often talk to themselves, silently and out loud, and their mouths may move as they repeat things they hear to themselves (known as sub-vocalizing) to ensure accurate processing of the input.

Head Position - Auditories will usually hold their heads in a balanced manner, looking straight in front of them. This gives them the best position to hear the most they can.

Face Color - Normal.

Language - Auditories use sound-related expressions when they speak, such as:

"I hear what you are saying."
"Sounds good to me."
"She dresses so loudly."
"I'm not hearing an answer."

"That is as clear as a bell."
"It doesn't have the ring of truth."
"Talk to me."

Refer to the list of predicates in the _Representational Systems_ chapter for additional words auditories would use.

Auditories often speak in dialog, as this is how they think and process information. Because of the way they process and record information, they also have the ability to recall conversations that took place years ago, word for word. They enjoy talking to themselves and frequently do so out loud.

Eye Movement - They will access memories as sounds and dialog, moving their eyes horizontally and to the left for something remembered and horizontally and to the right for something created. When they talk to themselves (either out loud or as internal dialog), their eyes will move down and to the left.

Refer to the _Eye Accessing Cues_ chapter for additional details.

Breathing - Auditories breathe deeply and regularly in a very pronounced rhythmic pattern, in a slower and more relaxed manner than visuals. Their breathing is mid-chest range. They may often sigh, a sign that they have just completed some sort of dialog with themselves.

Reading The Client - Representational Types

Dress - Auditories like to dress casually and somewhat subtly, they are often less bright and colorful then visuals. They prefer harmony so they will match their outfits well. Normally there will be less jewelry, or at least less ornate jewelry, although they will almost always have a wristwatch, usually one that ticks. As with visuals, if they find themselves in crisis, and their mind is preoccupied with discussions of how to handle the problem, their attention to their appearance might suffer and they may become less concerned about matching and neatness.

Thought Process - Auditories process all input as sounds, usually converted to a dialog that they can play back later for reference. Consequently, they think more slowly and deliberately, carefully finding the correct descriptive words to properly classify the data they are processing. Think of it as the speed of sound verses the speed of light (visuals). They must frequently discuss things with themselves to actually hear how they sound before committing them to memory or responding to them. Since they process all information as dialog, they find it very difficult to think and concentrate in a noisy room, as they are distracted by the other sounds which interfere with the information they are currently processing. They enjoy the fullness and richness of sound and prefer a sixteen piece orchestra to a solo guitar.

> Other - Auditories tend to love animals and may even prefer their company to that of humans. They get far more out of the purr of a kitten or the bark of a dog than others may. This may also be a reflection of their strong bond with nature, as they share a kinship with her. Consequently, they prefer living in the country, away from the endless din of the city (which they often find maddening), and closer to nature. In social interaction, auditories will find a small group in one corner of the room (usually other auditories), and converse with only them all evening. They find it impossible to tolerate distracting or overwhelming noises, and will leave the party if the band gets too loud.

Kinesthetics (touch)

Kinesthetics are the least common (excepting olfactories and gustatories), comprising about fifteen percent or less of the population. They base their reality on how things feel to them, how they sense things. They are very aware of texture, temperature, depth, etc. They think in terms of the way things feel and thus process information much less rapidly then the visual or the auditory, preferring to take information in as compared to a previous emotional or physical experience. Former President Bill Clinton is a good example of an kinesthetic.

> Speech - Kinesthetics speak excruciatingly slowly, with very deliberate words and often in a single monotone, picking each word for the way it describes how they feel about what they are discussing. Their conversation will

Reading The Client - Representational Types

appear somewhat broken to visuals and auditories, although other kinesthetics will not notice anything unusual about it. When they speak they must feel the words, so their speech is normally in a much lower voice, vibrating, and with a great deal of feeling. Again, they have to feel what they are talking about.

Gestures - Kinesthetics will come right up to you, practically nose to nose, when they converse. This makes many people uncomfortable, as they often violate a person's comfort zone. They cannot help it, however. They must feel your reaction to what they are saying; hearing and seeing just doesn't do it for them. When they are listening intently or speaking to a group they will often touch their chest or rub their chin. Their movements are very deliberate and calculated and they tend to walk very slowly, as if they were savoring the feeling of each step, the feel of each muscle moving. They prefer to touch things, and can often be very "hands-on". When you show them something or demonstrate something to them, hand it to them and let them feel it, or they may have no idea what you are talking about.

Head Position - Kinesthetics tend to tilt their head down, pulling their chin somewhat inward. In this way they can better feel their own breathing and reactions.

Face Color - Flushed

Language - Kinesthetics use feeling and emotion-related expressions when they speak, such as:

"I feel your pain."
"What is your gut reaction?"
"Do you sense this is correct?"
"I'm unable to grasp what you are telling me."
"That guy was hot."
"She is such a cold person."
"Ouch! That was a nasty comment."

Refer to the list of predicates in the _Representational Systems_ chapter for additional words kinesthetics would use. Kinesthetics will speak in feelings and emotions, as this is how they think and process information. Because of this, they may not remember the specifics of a situation, but they will vividly recall how they felt. For example, a kinesthetic may say, "I don't remember exactly what happened, but whenever I am around Sue I feel down and upset," recalling the emotions of an unpleasant incident of the past, but not the details. For this reason, it is very important that you never make a kinesthetic feel bad.

Eye Movement - Kinesthetics access all memories as feelings and emotions, and have only one movement, down and to the right.

Breathing - Kinesthetics breathe slowest of all, with very deep slow, belly breathing. As with everything they do, their breathing is

Reading The Client - Representational Types

deliberate and calculated, and it will appear that they are taking very deep breaths.

Dress - Kinesthetics dress very casually because it feels good. They respond to how comfortable their clothing is, and usually find formal clothes too confining and uncomfortable. Unmotivated by sight or harmony, they could care less if the outfits match (and even less if you were to object to their fashion sense). To them, an old, comfortable, broken-in pair of shoes is far better than tight, new, uncomfortable ones. Whatever they wear must feel good to them or it is perceived as unattractive.

Thought Process - As with their speech, kinesthetics' thought processes are very slow, deliberate and frequently excruciating to visuals and auditories. When thinking, they must apply feeling to everything they think about or recall. It may take them a very long time to decide exactly how they feel about a particular product or situation as they review all the possibilities and compare them to all previous physical and emotional experiences. When dealing with a kinesthetic you must be very patient. If they feel rushed, they prefer to leave for a safer, less-pressured haven.

Other - A kinesthetic loves to be home, secure and cuddled in front of a warm, comforting fire. They prefer this to being out at a party or other social function. Remember, they process everything as feelings, and very slowly.

When there is too much input, they are nervous and uncomfortable. Consequently, they dislike crowds. They always strive to be in touch with their feelings, and thus can be very moody, especially if they are having trouble reaching their feelings or feeling the current situation. They respond to touch, and enjoy a hug. When they shake hands, they will often hold your arm with their hand to feel you better.

Olfactory (smell) and Gustatory (taste)

As mentioned earlier, olfactory and gustatory are very uncommon types in our society, together comprising less then ten percent of the population. If you do encounter one, you will find that another representational system is quite prevalent, and they will respond well to it.

You will be able to identify an olfactory by their attention to fragrances and scents. Their speech will include such statements as:

> "This stinks."
> "Something is rotten in Denmark."
> "I've lost the scent."

A gustatory would use statements such as:

> "That is a bitter pill to swallow."
> "I am so mad I can taste it."
> "She has a sour personality."

Again, if you do encounter someone whose dominant representational system is olfactory or gustatory, find their

Reading The Client - Representational Types

next most prominent representational system and respond accordingly.

Once you have identified the client's dominant representational system you will know exactly how to respond to them. We will discuss this more in the Pacing chapters. However, this is not the only useful by-product of the identification of representational systems. By understanding the client's dominant representational system, you can begin to get an idea of how they think, process information and function. Additionally, this information provides you with a method to anticipate the tendencies of the client, making you better prepared to respond to their expectations. Below is a synopsis of the typical tendencies of each of the three major representational systems. It is important to note that this information, as in the case of the representational types, represents typical tendencies, and, since we are all individuals and not the product of a cookie-cutter, there are modifications, alterations and exceptions to all attempts to classify people. The intent is to provide a guide, a starting point to assist you in your interaction with your client.

Once again, olfactory and gustatory have been intentionally omitted.

Visual (sight)

Typically, the visual is an impatient person, driven by results and expecting them quickly. They object to being humored and prefer that you "show them the money". They respond best to things they can see, and the more colorful and clear they are the better. Never interrupt them, as they find this intolerable, and they must have your full and undivided attention when they speak to you even if it does not appear that they are giving your all of theirs. Things should be presented to the visual in a short, direct, to-the-point manner, with all of the fluff and glitz removed. When you speak to them, speak quickly and reach your point rapidly. If you are showing them something, allow them to look as long as they want; they are making a decision as they look.

Ask questions that elicit a visual response. Some questions you might ask a visual include:

> "How do you think this will look on you?"
> "Can you see yourself in this color?"
> "May I show you this new product?"

A visual will often seem harried or rushed. This is their way of reaching a decision, and is unlikely to be a reflection on you. Once they have made their decision, it is generally final and they will want to close the deal very quickly. Be especially aware of the visual's tendency to be a perfectionist; they will demand the same of any product and service you provide.

Auditory (sound)

The auditory finds comfort in an environment that has soothing background noises. Quiet music is especially appealing to them. They are quite proficient at interacting with people and will be "working" you at all times. Since they process information as dialog, they are very willing to hear both sides of a story and good at listening. However, you should never interrupt them, as you break the meter and rhythm of their thinking and the dissonance is very annoying to them. As they think and compare, they will do so in dialog, sometimes including you in their decision-making dialog session, "The red one is nice, don't you think, but the blue is more practical, wouldn't you agree?"Talk things over with them. This helps their thought process. However, be prepared for them to dominate the conversation and over-explain things. Let them. When you speak to them, use clear, descriptive words, speaking at the same rate and speed that they do. Metaphors are easily understood by the auditory and they enjoy getting the point, so introduce metaphors in your conversation whenever possible.

Ask questions that elicit auditory responses. Some questions you might ask an auditory include:

"How does that sound?"
"Can't you just hear what they are saying when you enter the room?"
"Does this ring a bell?"

Avoid presenting an auditory with imagery, as they will not understand it. Direct all of your explanations to things involving sound. Remember, they think in dialog, and will often ask others to enter the dialog of their decision-making process, thus they are easily talked into and out of things by those involved in the dialog.

Kinesthetics (touch)

Kinesthetics typically possess great negotiation skills, so be prepared to bargain with them. However, as brilliant business people they will understand your need to make a profit. They can easily and quickly detect when they are being manipulated and will cut through it to get to the heart of the matter. Their slowness to react makes them excellent leaders, although they can often be frustrating as clients, because they will wait,
ponder and consider before leaping.

There are two types of kinesthetics, internal and

external. The internal puts a great deal of emphasis on how people and places make them feel inside, "I have a bad feeling about this." The external, on the other hand, tends to be very touchy, with their hands on everything, including the people they are talking to.

Kinesthetics will wait patiently and listen intently to everything you say, as they get a feeling about you. Once they have decided how you feel to them, they will respond accordingly, and it is difficult to alter that feeling. They are very susceptible to mood swings, as they respond emotionally to their feelings.

Visual things simply do not impress them, they go by how things feel to them. When offering them a product or service, let them physically sample what it will feel like. They are even more influenced by metaphor then auditories, so use metaphor frequently, remembering always to phrase your statements and questions in terms of feelings.

Ask questions that elicit kinesthetic responses. Some questions and comments you might make to a kinesthetic include:

"How does that feel?"
"This will make your skin smooth and soft."
"Notice how relaxed this makes you feel?"

Kinesthetics are known to be human lie-detectors and can tell if they are being told something that is untrue. Also, be sure to answer all of their questions prior to their purchase, as they are very prone to buyer's remorse. Take all the time you need to explain things, as they are very patient and will give you the opportunity to sell them over and over again. Remember that they are motivated by feeling, so add as much emotion to the product or service as you can. Do everything you can to saturate their emotions and their sense of feeling.

Reading The Client - Representational Types

With the identification of a client's representational system we have a better understanding of their reality and how they process information. In this way we can organize and direct our responses in the language they will understand. This is an important aspect of Mind Aesthetics® and a necessary step in the process of influence and persuasion.

10
Eye Accessing Cues

Eye accessing cues offer another opportunity for us to determine what representational system is being accessed by the client as information is processed. By observing the eye movements of a person while they are actively retrieving information from their subconscious mind, we can determine what representational system they are using in the accessing of that information, and accordingly what representational system was dominant at the time that the information was originally programmed into their subconscious. Additionally, it can show us if the information is actually being retrieved or is being spontaneously created in response to the question.

The diagram in Fig. 4 represents a person whom you face. When you ask them a question, observe carefully as they are responding (retrieving information from their subconscious mind). You can look at the position of their eyes to determine, with some degree of accuracy, the representational system they are using as they retrieve that information.

Make-Up Their Mind

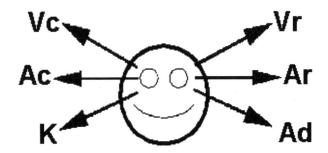

Fig. 4: Eye Accessing Movements

Vc - Visually Constructed: Indicates the person is seeing images of things never before seen, or seeing things differently than they were seen before.
Questions that can elicit this response include: "What would you look like with half of your face painted orange?" or "What would a horse with purple spots look like dancing?" These questions will force the person to visualize something they have never seen before, resulting in a visually constructed image.

Ac - Auditory Constructed: Hearing sounds never heard before.
Questions that would elicit this response include: "What would the sound of the ocean be like in reverse?" or "What would a bird sound like singing the words to the Beatles' song, *Yesterday*?" Questions of

Eye Accessing Cues

this type will force the person to create the sound in response to the inquiry.

K - Kinesthetic: Feeling emotions, tactile (sense of touch) sensations or proprioceptive feeling (the sensation of muscle movement). Questions that would elicit this response include: "What does it feel like to walk up stairs?" or "Is the temperature comfortable for you right now?" These questions will force the person to retrieve previously stored kinesthetic information from their subconscious mind.

Vr - Visual Remembered: Seeing images of things that have been seen before, and seeing them exactly the way they were originally seen. Questions that would elicit this response include: "What color is your car?" or "Can you visualize the American Flag?" These questions force the person to retrieve the visual images stored in their subconscious mind.

Ar - Auditory Remembered: Remembering sounds that have been heard before exactly the way they were previously programmed into the subconscious. Questions that would elicit this response include: "What was the last question I asked you?" or "How does your favorite song go?" Such questions require the person to retrieve the audio information stored in their subconscious programming to rehear the information.

Ad - Auditory Digital: Talking to oneself. Questions that would elicit this response include: "Say your name to yourself," or "Recite the Pledge of Allegiance to the Flag." This forces the person to retrieve the audio information from their subconscious mind, permitting them to respond to what they have been asked.

Blank Stare - A blank stare is generally visual, either constructed or remembered.

This system is not foolproof, but it is another tool that can be used to determine how the client thinks and processes information, and to assist you in identifying the representational systems the client is accessing, as well as determining if the information they are providing is from a memory or is being created spontaneously.

11
Representational System Pacing

Undoubtedly the best and fastest way to build rapport is *pacing*, or emulating the behavior of the client. The client sets the pace and you follow their lead. In other words, you stay with the client. Pacing is the first stage, during which the client is the leader and you must follow them. It is very important that you allow yourself to be led during this phase. Once rapport has been established, you will take over the lead and the client will follow you.

We begin by pacing the client's dominant representational system. By following the steps in the previous chapters we have successfully identified this, so this pacing technique involves emulating the client's dominant representational system, and communicating with them in their own language. For example, let us suppose that we have identified our client as being a visual. We know this because we have observed that the client speaks very fast, in bursts of often unfinished sentences, holding their head up high and using statements like, "You have to see this" and "I get the picture" while moving their hands and body about actively as they speak in a very animated manner. They move their eyes upwards when accessing information or responding to a question that requires thought, and they are dressed in brightly colored clothes that match perfectly. Yes, you can be quite certain that this client is visual.

Now you pace this client's dominant representational system by beginning to act like a visual, adopting the same characteristics as a visual, emulating so far as you can the typical behavior of a visual as previously described, and particularly the behavior of *this* visual, which may differ in some ways from the profile.

One of the best ways to begin is by pacing their language, their words. In other words, by following their verbal cues. Although the things we actually say, or the words we use, only account for about seven percent of how we communicate, this is an excellent way to start building rapport. Moreover, it is absolutely essential that we pace the client's verbal communication by using their dominant representational system's word types if we are to have any verbal interaction with them, such as describing and selling a product or service we expect them to buy, or even just engaging in casual conversation.

Pacing their words in this way is accompanied by simply following the client's choice of predicates. Refer back to the list of predicates provided above for reference. Our visual, for example, will understand things that you express to him visually. When describing a product to the visual, explain how it will *look* on them, how others will *see* them when they use it, how their *appearance* will improve.

Make sure you use lots of visual descriptions in everything you talk about to your visual client, and respond in visuals as well, "Oh, I see what you mean." This establishes good communication and understanding and begins the rapport-building process. It is perfectly alright to mix predicates, if necessary. For example, if you were giving our visual client a massage, you might say, "*See* how relaxed you feel" or "*Look* how the tension is leaving your muscles."

Always use the words that your clients will understand. Remember, we all communicate in the language that we are most comfortable with, and we understand best in the same language. The situation can be compared to speaking to a native of France, who understands English as well. If he had a choice of conversing in English or French, which do you think he would choose? Obviously, French. Even though he can understand English, he must translate the English words into French to fully understand what you are telling him, and much is lost in the translation. The same is true of our clients. Our visual client may understand things spoken in auditory or kinesthetic terms, but they must first translate them into visual terms. In some cases, such as the use of the word "tight", translation is ineffective, and some of the meaning is lost.

Try to employ the same vocabulary as the client. Speak to them on their level. Of course, if they are talking about something very technical in a field that you are not familiar with, avoid trying to fake it, it will not work. In these situations, use words that you are comfortable with and that you fully understand so that you express yourself properly. Your confidence in the words you have chosen will echo in your speech and serve the same purpose. If the client is speaking below your vocabulary level, adjust your speech so that you are conversing on the same level.

Let us look at some examples of well-structured and poorly-structured responses to illustrate the process more clearly:

You hear: "I don't *see* what she *sees* in him."
Well structured response:
"*Obviously* it is a mismatch"

Make-Up Their Mind

Poorly structured response:
> "I *hear* they are planning to get married."

You hear: "Can we *discuss* this here?"
Well structured response:
> "Sure, let's *talk* about it."
Poorly structured response:
> "I don't *see* why not."

You hear: "This project is going to be rough ... "
Well structured response:
> "I had a *feeling* ... "
Poorly structured response:
> "*Imagine* if they gave us less time."

You hear: "This wine is *delicious*!"
Well structured response:
> "Yes, it *tastes* wonderful!"
Poorly structured response:
> "It's *clearly* a good vintage!"
You hear: "You could *smell* the fear when they mentioned layoffs."
Well structured response:
> "It *spoiled* my day, and it *reeks* of politics."
Poorly structured response:
> "I *heard* that was only a rumor."

We continue to pace their verbal communication by using their dominant representational system's predicates throughout all of the other techniques, especially when we begin to lead.

12
Mirroring and Matching

Since most of our communication - fifty-five percent or more - involves non-verbal communication, the best method of pacing is that of *mirroring and matching*. Mirroring and matching is based on the theory that if a behavior is modeled exactly, it can be duplicated by anyone. In other words, any behavior that one person engages in can be successfully reproduced by another. We do this on the simplest level from the time we are born. This is the way in which we learn to walk and talk.

Mirroring and matching is reflecting the client's behavior, such as body position, eye movement, breathing, etc., back to them. It might be argued that all of the pacing methods involve mirroring and matching to some degree, but for the sake of clarity I prefer to reserve the term to refer to the pacing of the client's non-verbal communication.

Mirroring non-verbal communication, particularly the replication of breathing patterns, is an extremely powerful and effective way to rapidly build, maintain and strengthen rapport. The reason for this is probably because we all like ourselves, and we tend to accept naturally that part of others that reminds us of ourselves. We feel comfortable with someone just like us. Thus, when we mirror and match a client, we are entering their world as a reproduction of themselves. This can be called *psychological reciprocity*.

Mirroring and matching builds rapport. This is a fact, and the reverse is equally true - people in rapport will automatically mirror and match each other. We have all had the experience of listening to someone and finding ourselves nodding as they nod or shaking our head at the same time they do, automatically, without realizing we are doing it, or being seated and talking with someone and standing up when they do without consciously thinking about standing.

We can observe rapport in others, as well. For example, look at two people walking. If they are in rapport they will take the steps of the same size, and lead with the same foot. When they climb stairs, they will do so with the same pace and footing, and depending on the depth of their rapport, they may even swing their arms the same way. As a matter of fact, if we were to observe these two people walking from the side, they would appear as only one person, as their movements would be so precisely the same.

Study two people who are in love. They are certainly in deep rapport. You will notice that when they speak to each other they do so in the same tempo and tone of voice. Their mannerisms and gestures are the same, as are their facial expressions. They express the same emotions in the same way. In a restaurant, they will reach for their glass of wine at about the same moment. They will have a slightly glazed look to their eyes, characteristic of the hypnoidal stage of the hypnotic state.

Watch a group of friends who are watching a football game on TV together. Those in rapport will drink their beers and reach for the chips at the same time.

Mirroring and Matching

Watch as one person tells a story to another with whom they are in rapport. You will see that as the teller's face and emotions change, the listener's face and emotions will change also, exactly matching those of the teller. When people are in rapport, their communication takes on a cadence, with behaviors, gestures, and words matching one another in a smooth, easy, rhythmic pattern.

It is an amazing phenomenon. Studies have shown that women in the same dormitory will eventually find that their periods - their menstrual cycles - have actually synchronized after several months if they are in rapport. Those not in rapport with the others will not experience this, demonstrating another aspect of mirroring and matching, the fact that those who do not share rapport typically find themselves in contrast and conflict with each other. They may make the statement, "I don't know why, I just don't like her."

However, rapport is the preferred state, and one which even nature seems to strive towards. If we were to fill a room with grandfather clocks, and all of the pendulums were started in different rhythms, in a short time they would all synchronize until they were all swinging in the same time and in the same way. This leads me to believe that nature tends to favor balance. Certainly, with people, congruency is favored over dissonance, and mirroring and matching illustrates this
fact most effectively.

One of the most interesting demonstrations of mirroring and matching that occurs in people is beyond their control! We all have noticed how people who have been married or together for a very long time, or who have been friends for a very long time eventually begin to resemble each other. Well, there is actually a firm basis for this that has been corroborated by scientific research. It has to do with rapport, mirroring and matching and the way our subconscious mind controls the involuntary muscles in our body. These people share a very strong degree of rapport, and their subconscious mind, in an effort to maintain and strengthen that rapport, begins to mirror and match the other person. Remember that our subconscious mind is also always striving for rapport. It works to continue and increase the rapport by emulating behaviors and mannerisms, habits, speech patterns, even voice, (people who have been together for a long time often adopt each others verbal characteristics and begin to sound alike when they speak). But it goes even further than that. Since our subconscious mind has control over the voluntary and involuntary muscles in our body, it actually begins to alter and modify the facial muscles, reshaping the face to further mirror the other person's until they begin to resemble each other. Astounding! The longer they are together, the more they will tend to look alike, as each person's subconscious mind continues to work toward resembling (mirroring) the other. This alone certainly validates the enormous importance of Mind Aesthetics®.

Let's discuss how we use mirroring and matching as an intricate aspect of the rapport-building process. The simplicity of it is that to build rapport using mirroring and matching is merely a matter of observing and reflecting the client's non-verbal cues. We have already learned how to identify many of these cues when we studied representational systems. Once we have chosen a characteristic, we then *match* it and *mirror* it back to them, so that they see themselves in us. This is an extremely important rapport-building skill, so we will spend an appropriate amount of time on it.

Body Position

We can mirror and match body position and movement. Observe the way the client is standing

Mirroring and Matching

or sitting, paying particular attention to the details of their position.

Hands: Observe the location of the hands. Notice if they are on their lap, or by their side, if the palms are up or down. If the fingers are relaxed, crossed or clenched in a fist. If they are clasped to each other. If they are moving or at rest. If they are on their face, etc.

Arms: Notice if the arms are crossed or by their sides. If they are bent at the elbow. If one hand is clasping the opposite arm. If they are still or mobile.

Shoulders: Notice if the shoulders are slumped or erect. If they are tilted back or forward. If they are tilted so that one is lower than the other. If they are dropped.

Neck and Head: Observe if the head is tilted up or down, or to either side. If the chin is raised or lowered. If the brow is wrinkled or relaxed. If the jaw is stuck out or drawn back. If the neck is twisted.

Torso and Hips: Notice how the client is sitting. If the torso is twisted or straight. If they are sitting back on the chair or at the front edge. If their hips are even or slouched to one side. If the chest is concave or stuck out. If their back is arched or straight. If they are leaning to one side or standing perfectly erect.

Legs: Observe if the knees are bent or straight. If the legs are crossed. If they are crossed, notice at which point, above or below the knee. If they are leaning their arms or resting their hands on their thighs. If they are close together or spread apart.

Ankles, Feet and Toes: Notice if the ankles are bent or straight. If the feet are flat on the floor or lifted up. If the toes are pointed towards or away from each other. If the feet are touching each other or separated. If the toes are bent or straight.

Overall: Observe if they are standing, sitting, leaning, etc. If they have shifted their weight to one foot or the other. If they are erect or hunched.

Once you have completely identified the position of every external part of the body, assume exactly the same position, maintaining right and left just as the client does. Do this in graceful movements until your position is precisely the same as theirs. If your vision is obscured by a table or desk, match the part you can see exactly and then, based on what you can see, imagine how the obscured limbs are likely to be positioned and assume that posture.

Body Movements: In the course of your interaction with the client, they will undoubtedly make some change in their position, moving one or many parts of their body. To handle this properly you should wait a few seconds, and then, very gracefully and gradually, make the same changes to your limbs and body so that you once again assume the same position.

It is important that you wait a few seconds (no more than thirty or forty-five) before you adjust your posture. The reason for the delay is to avoid exposing your intent, because, just as surely and easily as mirroring and matching can build rapport, if you were to "get caught" or for any reason give the client the impression that you are mocking them, the rapport will be broken. Once rapport is lost in this way it is very difficult to recover. However, you will be surprised to find how deliberately you can mirror and match someone, with very bold movements, without them realizing what you are doing. They do not expect it, and their mind is preoccupied with the other things that are happening. All that they will realize is that they feel very comfortable around you and that there is something about you that they like very much, although they cannot put their finger on it.

Facial Expression

We can mirror and match facial expressions. Observe the way the client expresses him or herself facially. They may show joy when talking about something that recalls a pleasant memory. Some people squint when they are angry or display a sorrowful expression when accessing a hurtful memory. Look at their lips. They may be frowning or smiling, or simply have a plain or blank expression. Their lips may be tight or relaxed, parted or pressed tightly closed. Their cheeks may be relaxed or drawn up. Eyebrows may be lifted or pushed down. Match your facial expression to theirs, pacing them as they change. Watch their eyes, too. If they are constantly looking at the floor or the ceiling, distracted and avoiding looking at you or failing to make eye contact, you must regain their attention and bring their focus back to you as quickly as you can.

Eye Movement

You should always pay close attention to the eyes. When the client makes eye contact with you, return it the same amount of time. Observe how they are moving their eyes and match these movements. A very powerful rapport-builder is to match the client's blinking, or to time your blinking exactly to theirs so that when they blink, you blink, with the same rate, rhythm and frequency. Normally we do not consciously notice someone's blinking, unless there is something about it that is unusual, such as a tic or some other abnormal characteristic. However, the subconscious mind notices everything. In fact, every thought, sight, sound, smell and taste you have ever experienced is recorded by the subconscious mind regardless of the degree of conscious attention you have given it, if any at all. This is why people who have witnessed a crime, such as a robbery, can accurately recall details such as a license plate number when in hypnosis, even when they do not realize what they have seen. Consequently, the client's subconscious mind will notice very quickly that your blinking is synchronized and this will build rapport quite rapidly, and covertly. This makes mirroring and matching of the blinking pattern one of the more powerful rapport-builders.

Mirroring and Matching

Emotional State

Another extremely powerful rapport-builder is to mirror and match the client's emotional state. If they are *angry*, appear to express the same emotion. If they shout, raise your voice too. Remember that no one likes to suffer alone, and you will build rapport by sharing the way they feel, by empathizing with them. Similarly, if they are happy and you are not, it will alienate you from them, as they will feel that you are bringing them down.

To put this in a different context, think of how people react to a common goal or enemy. Nothing bonds people more closely, even when they are very different. The terrorist attack on the United States on September 11, 2001 certainly demonstrates this dramatically. Immediately after the tragedy, people - even those normally in opposition to one another - forgot their differences, and entered rapport with each other, drawn together by a common enemy and a common goal. For a time, everyone was "one of us". Such is the power of rapport.

Further on the subject of mirroring and matching the client's emotional state, it is important to note that once you are in rapport, you will actually be able to change their emotional state, and lead them to a calmer, more relaxed, happier one. This is a very important
aspect of Mind Aesthetics®, and we will study this in depth when we discuss leading.

Speech Patterns

We can mirror and match the client's speech. That is the speed, pace, volume, tone, intensity, etc. of their speech. Listen carefully to the characteristics of the client's voice as they speak, and adjust your speech so that you are responding to them with the same tempo, timbre, volume, etc. - the same qualities of voice. If they change their face while speaking, or tilt their head, you should do the same. Observe carefully how they phrase their sentences and where they take breaths. Notice if they raise the syllables on the end, or fade out as they finish a thought. Mirror and match all of the qualities of their speech, pacing them as they change. They may get louder when making a point or softer when saying something that saddens them.

It is important to understand that our purpose here is to match the *qualities* of their speech as opposed to their voice. It is not our intention to become impressionists or mimics. In fact, unless you have a natural talent as an impressionist, they will notice what you are trying to do and become quite insulted, breaking rapport instantly. So it is important that you understand that your goal here is to match the qualities of their voice and avoid attempting to impersonate them.

Breathing

This brings us to breathing. By far the absolute best, and quickest way to build instant rapport with a client is to match their breathing pattern. That is, when they inhale, you inhale, when they exhale, you

Mirroring and Matching

exhale. Breathing, as with blinking, is something we do not normally focus conscious attention on, but once again, our subconscious mind, which controls our breathing, is very aware of and sensitive to how a person breathes, and will quickly see the replication and synchronization. Rapport will follow almost immediately.

Mirroring and matching one's breathing pattern can be a bit tricky. You must be very observant to determine how someone is breathing, and it is especially difficult to observe with certain representational types. Besides, it would often be inappropriate to stare at your client's chest, and this would be likely to make them quite uncomfortable. However, there is a way to determine the client's breathing pattern without damaging rapport or risking embarrassment or an uncomfortable situation. To do this, pay close attention to how the client is speaking. We all exhale as we speak and inhale at the end of a sentence or a phrase. If the client's breathing pattern changes during the conversation, you must pace them, changing yours as well.

When you are able to match the client's breathing, all of the other things -eye movements, body position, facial expressions, etc. - will fall into place automatically. Thus we must strive to mirror and match the breathing pattern. It may be the most difficult technique to learn, but it is the most effective, so direct as much effort as you can to mirroring and matching the client's breathing.

13
Verbal Pacing

Another very powerful pacing method is to verbally pace the client. This differs from pacing the client's verbal communication (using predicates of the client's dominant representational system) in that when verbally pacing the client, we are eliciting a particular response from them. The response we are seeking is "yes". We obtain this response by asking the client questions they can only answer "yes" to, and by making statements that the client can only agree with. By developing this "yes" flow, this chain of "yeses", the client will become agreeable. This is because we can only think in affirmatives. Our mind only understands positive concepts. When we are presented with a negative, our mind must first translate it into a positive before we can even conceive of the concept of the reverse. Once the information has been converted to a positive, our mind can then determine the intention and modify the information to reflect the actual meaning.

For example, if I were to tell you:

Don't forget that Friday is the big meeting.

Your mind will understand this as:

~~Don't~~ *forget that Friday is the big meeting.*

The "don't" will be dropped. Now that you understand what *to* do, *(Forget that Friday is the big meeting,* a positive) your mind can, if it chooses, negate the statement and rephrase it, perhaps as:

Remember that Friday is the big meeting.

However, your mind may stop before the negation process is complete, and there are many psychological and external factors that can conceivably cause this to happen. When this occurs, it will simply ignore the negative and accept the statement as it first understood it.

This brings us to a very important point. Always, *always*, speak in positive terms. You should remove words like:

Shouldn't
Can't
Won't

and especially

Don't

from your vocabulary. I call "don't" *the invisible word,* because when you use it, the listener will ignore it and only hear the rest of the statement. For example, how many times have you told a child, "Don't drop that" and what happens? The object falls immediately to the floor. Right? Now, this is not because the child is being disobedient. Quite the contrary. In fact he is doing exactly what you told him to do *as he understood it.* His mind did not understand the word "don't", and, realizing that you were in authority and that he must respond to you quickly and without question, he reacted to

Verbal Pacing

what he understood you had said, before his mind could negate and rephrase the statement. (As an interesting side note, in this situation, you probably reprimanded or punished the child. This creates confusion, as the child fails to understand why he was being punished for doing what he was told to do. Irreconcilable contradictions such as this are the roots of more serious psychological concerns in the future.)

Another example: You are at the mall with a friend. In the mall there is a shop which sells expensive figurines that you particularly like. You and your friend enter the store, in which there are several other patrons. As you are looking at a particularly attractive and expensive piece, the clerk, concerned about a possible accident in the crowded store, comes over to you and sternly says, "Don't touch that!" Immediately, the muscles in your arm tense up and your hand begins to move toward the statue as if to reach for it, until you are able to regain control and pull your arm back. Defiance? No. It is just timing. The muscular reaction to the instruction "~~Don't~~ touch that!" (understood as "Touch that!") was simply a few milliseconds faster then the translated final instruction, "Leave that alone!" and in those few milliseconds your body began to do what it was told. This is an interesting phenomenon.

A TV commercial that shouts, "Don't touch that dial", actually will get you wondering what else is on right now as it elicits the reaction, "Funny, I wasn't even thinking about changing the channel . . . until now."

Read the following statement:

Don't look at the opposite page.

You see!

Make-Up Their Mind

Here is another exercise you can try that will drive the point home, and hopefully motivate you further to get rid of those negatives. This exercise requires the participation of a friend or spouse, so make sure that he or she is willing to cooperate with you.

Ask your subject to sit at a table and follow all of your instructions. Have a watch with a second hand available. Place an object on the table in front of the subject. Give the subject the following instructions:

1. "Lift the object five inches above the table."
2. "Move the object to your left."
3. "Grasp the object with your right hand and move it to your left."
4. "Pick a spot on the object and focus your attention on it."

Give as many positively worded instructions as you wish. As you give each instruction, use your watch to time how long it takes for them to respond to your instruction.

Next, give the subject a series of negatively worded instructions such as:

1. "Move the object anywhere except not to the right."
2. "Lift the object no more than eight inches."
3. "Grasp the object in the hand that is not the right hand."
4. "Touch the object without using either foot."

Observe as they struggle with the negatives, often failing to follow your instructions.

The important point here is that a very necessary skill you must develop is the elimination of as many negative statements from your speech as possible. You should do this

Verbal Pacing

today. Right now. It will help you in your interaction with your clients, co-workers, friends and family. It will help you in life in general. So begin right now and drop those negatives from your everyday speech. This may seem a bit awkward at first, as in our society we word many statements negatively, but the reward is well worth any effort.

Another important consideration when verbally pacing is to maintain simultaneous pacing of the client's dominant representational system's predicates. In other words, remember to phrase your questions and statements using terminology that the client will understand. This further bypasses any conscious interference with the verbal pacing process that could result during the translation process.

Verbal pacing is especially useful in actual selling. For example, consider the following dialogue:

Nail Tech: "My, it is a beautiful day today, isn't it?"

Mrs. Smith: "Sure is. It's about time it stopped raining." [YES]

Nail Tech: "Wow, you certainly do look good in this color."

Mrs. Smith: "Yes, I do!" [YES]

Nail Tech: "That party on Saturday, is it important?"

Mrs. Smith: "Oh yes, it's for John's boss" [YES]

Nail Tech: "I guess you had better look your best."

Mrs. Smith:	"You know it!"	**[YES]**
Nail Tech:	"You think you should take some home with you?"	
Mrs. Smith:	"Yes, you had better give me two bottles."	**[YES]**

As this dialogue illustrates, developing a chain of "yes" answers is the key to eliciting a positive response to your goal question(s). The client becomes more comfortable with saying "yes" after she has done so a few times.

Let us consider some other examples of verbal pacing. Obviously, when you verbally pace your client, you must know that the answer is "yes" before you ask the question or make the statement. This is very important. One "no" answer will break the chain and require that you begin a new "yes" series. It is an extremely easy thing to do, and it is unnecessary for you to know anything at all about the client beforehand. Just be observant and you will find that many opportunities for positive statements and questions will present themselves.

For example, you can look at your client and notice her jewelry. Then you can make a statement such as:

"My, that is a beautiful ring you have on."

She will, of course, agree. She would not be wearing it if she did not think it was attractive. Basically, the process of verbal pacing is as simple as that. You might look in the appointment book and see that it has been two weeks since the client's last appointment, and say:

"It has been about two weeks since your last appointment, hasn't it?"

Verbal Pacing

Again you will receive an affirmative response. The intent, once again, is to put together a chain of "yes" answers, to keep their head nodding "yes". Knowing that the client has just gotten a new car that he really loves, you might say:

"I was thinking of buying a BMW, is it a good car?"

Always eliciting that "yes" answer.

Let us suppose that you are unable to come up with any questions. In this situation, keep it simple. Simplicity is often the best way to go. Consider the date, or the weather:

"It sure is raining!"

or

"Today is Thursday, isn't it?"

You get the idea. By presenting the client with questions and statements that can only be answered positively, the series of yes answers will establish a positive, agreeable atmosphere, and the client will tend to express agreement with you even about things they may not actually agree with. Remember, it is much easier for the client to agree than to disagree. Congruency is always favored over dissonance. Always.

14
Other Pacing Methods

Any quality or characteristic of the client can be paced. We have discussed pacing verbal and non-verbal communication. Other, albeit more abstract, qualities that can be paced include belief systems, values and experience. For example, if a client plays golf, and chooses to talk about it, you can ask questions, contribute your limited knowledge and encourage the discussion even if you are not a golfer, following the client as far as they wish to go with the topic.

At times this process requires a great deal of diplomacy, self control and finesse. For example, suppose a client comes to you and begins to talk about politics, particularly, for example, their ardent support of the death penalty, something to which you are diametrically opposed. At this point you have to make a decision. If your intention is to argue your point and try to force your opinion on the client, (which, by the way, you will not be able to do), then forget about rapport-building and buy a soapbox. If, however, your desire is to build rapport with the client, and to use that rapport to persuade and influence the client (perhaps even ultimately leading them toward your point of view), thus reaching your goal of selling them products

Make-Up Their Mind

or services, and generating more business from them, as well as reaching inside their mind and making them feel beautiful, then continue using the Mind Aesthetics® techniques and achieve your objective.

The point I am making is that you must never lose sight of your primary goal, and this may take a little, or a great deal, of tongue-biting. When it does, just gulp it down and recall the techniques that you have learned, with a clear and level head. After they have left, and you are counting your money, you can think whatever you want. However, while they are there, you must swallow your pride and appear to agree with the client, never tipping your hand or exposing your true feelings. This is not to say that you should compromise your morals or ethics, only that it is prudent to keep them to yourself at times.

You could pace the client's experience. For example, suppose you know, or learn through your conversation with them, that they have children. You could pace this experience by encouraging the client to talk about them and referencing your own children and similar experiences you have had, always empathizing and seeming to agree with the client, and most importantly, never appearing insincere.

By using a variety of pacing methods, you will rapidly build and maintain rapport. Remember, rapport is dynamic, and constantly changing. It is your responsibility to continue strengthening it, or at the very least, maintaining it, so you must always be pacing or leading to continue the state. Once you are in deep rapport with the client, staying in rapport becomes easier, as processes such as mirroring and matching, which are deliberate at first, become automatic once rapport has been achieved. In this way, rapport attempts to replicate itself, although you must be aware if the state begins to deteriorate, usually because of some external interruption or distraction.

Other Pacing Methods

We must consider one more issue when mirroring, matching and pacing. That is a person's comfort zone, the area around them that they consider sacred. You must never violate this zone. Think of how you feel when someone stands too close to you. You become uncomfortable and uneasy and eager to get away from them. No matter what they are talking about, you are thinking, "I've got to get away from here." Every person's comfort zone is different, so a standard is difficult to reach. However, if you are standing near someone and they step back, you have probably violated their comfort zone.

Finally, when establishing rapport, it is very important to become a good listener. People like to talk about themselves, and the more you let them, and listen to them, the better they will feel, and the easier it will be to enter rapport with them. Interestingly, as you concentrate on pacing, mirroring and matching their cues, the effort you are using will actually give you the appearance of being a good listener, automatically.

Effective pacing, mirroring and matching can be best summed up as replicating what a person does (movements, posture, speech, language etc.), and how they do it (thought process, and strategies), while understanding why they do it and respecting their principals, beliefs and comfort zone.

It now becomes even more clear how sensory acuity plays an indispensable role in establishing rapport. During the process you must be keenly aware of:

1. Breathing patterns.
2. Body position and movements.
3. Facial expressions.
4. Language patterns.
5. Eye movements.
6. Representational systems being accessed.
7. Gestures and limb movement.

8. Emotional state.
9. Thought patterns and processes.
10. Comfort zone.

And that is not all. Each of these attributes and cues are dynamic, and change from minute to minute. As this occurs, you must change to match them too. This is a lot to ask our conscious mind to do. Consequently, it is best to develop the skill of establishing rapport by practicing often and with attention. Eventually this will become a function of your subconscious mind. In this way, you will be reading the cues, pacing and mirroring and matching, from a subconscious level all of the time. You will be amazed and delighted by how different your interaction with clients will be, and by how much more influence you will have when you are able to establish instant rapport with them effortlessly.

15
Calibration and Leading

Let us review the steps that we have learned up to this point:

1. We have learned how to prepare ourselves by entering the Zone.
2. We have learned how to identify the client's dominant representational system by listening to the predicates, comparing them to the typical representational types and observing their verbal and non-verbal cues.
3. We have learned how to enter rapport by pacing their verbal representational language and mirroring and matching their non-verbal communications.
4. We have learned how to strengthen rapport by verbally pacing the client.

We will now learn how to test the depth of that rapport. Technically, the process is called *calibration*. Calibration is the skill of learning to read the unconscious, non-verbal responses of the client, and it is an excellent way

Make-Up Their Mind

to test to see if you are in rapport with someone. It refers to observing the changes in a person as they react to your communication. Sensory acuity is required for this skill (see chapter on <u>Sensory Acuity</u>).

As someone enters rapport with you, certain physiological changes begin to take place. The color in their face and hands intensifies, and subtle changes can be observed in their eyes, the muscles around the eyes, their lower lip and their breathing. The legs and chest develop a slight tingling or a feeling of expectation or anticipation immediately before the color change in the face and hands. The changes take place in both people as they reach rapport, so you can look for them in yourself as well. Frequently, as a person enters rapport, the content of their speech will reflect this. They may begin to include statements, such as "you, my dear friend," or "I can trust you," or "we've been friends for a long time, haven't we?" They may actually begin to use words like "agreement", "harmony", "faith" and "trust," in their speech when referring to you. They may actually use the word "rapport".

As we watch for these subtle changes, we can perform a more decisive test for the presence of rapport. It involves *leading*. Leading is the reverse of pacing, that is, you now initiate the non-verbal communication and the client follows your lead. For the purpose of testing the depth of rapport, we lead the client simply by reversing the mirroring and matching process, and observe if they mirror and match us. For example, you can change the position of your arm or hand, cross your legs (or uncross them), tilt your head in a different way, etc. Within a few seconds, the client in rapport will follow your lead and make the same changes, assuming your position exactly, without even realizing that they have done so. This is because, now that you are in rapport, the mirroring and matching process exists in both parties.

Calibration and Leading

With rapport present, the continued mirroring and matching, from either or both parties, will maintain the rapport and even strengthen it. If at any point after rapport has been established you become aware of it becoming fragile, simply assume the role of follower and begin the pacing process once again. This will reestablish the depth of rapport very rapidly.

The same is true if the client does not follow your lead and you determine that rapport is not present. Something may have distracted the client and drawn them out of rapport. If the client fails to follow your lead, just begin pacing them once again, perhaps using some of the pacing techniques that you may have omitted in the first attempt, and proceed again to establish rapport.

As with all skills, the more you practice the better you will become. I urge you to practice your rapport-building skills everywhere you go, with friends, strangers, family, everyone. Here is an interesting exercise you can use when out at a bar or restaurant to test the depth of your rapport. It is great because it is fun while at the same time you are practicing without the possibility of negative effects if you are initially unsuccessful.

Here's what you do:

> Go out to a bar or restaurant with a friend. As you have a drink or eat, use all of your pacing and mirroring and matching techniques to establish rapport. Use your sensory acuity skills to read the non-verbal cues and include predicates in your conversation. Practice your observation skills as well. In particular, watch your subject's glass or cup. Make sure you do not empty yours first. Wait till the subject's cup or glass is empty, and very obviously and deliberately take a sip from yours. If you are in rapport your subject will lift his glass or cup, and,

realizing it is empty, look for a server to order another drink.

Try it, you will be amazed to find it works!

With rapport established, we can lead the client that we have been pacing in any way. This is especially important with respect to the client's physical, emotional and mental state. This is among the most important aspects of the Mind Aesthetics® application; your ability to improve the client's condition. Consider the client who arrives at your salon stressed, tense and mentally fatigued. After establishing rapport with them, you will be able to lead them to a state of calm relaxation and mental rejuvenation, by projecting these characteristics and offering suggestions to change their state, as we will now see.

16
The Magic

Once you are certain that you are in rapport, the real magic behind Mind Aesthetics® begins. We are now ready to take the next step in our carefully choreographed dance of persuasion, the next phase in the application of Mind Aesthetics®: that of reaching our desired goal of persuading and influencing the client and, more importantly, making them feel beautiful inside.

Now that we have established rapport with the client, we have entered the client's world. They trust us. We are, so to speak, inside the client's head. When we are inside the client's head in this way, we have a tremendous power in our ability to influence them. That trust, that rapport, gives us the power to make them happy or sad. To make them calm or nervous. To make them want to come back in the future. To make them want to send others to see us. Even to make them want to purchase products and services. In short, once we have entered the client's reality through the building of rapport we have the power to make them feel beautiful inside as well as out. All of the power of influence and suggestion that we now have over the client can only lead to one thing; by properly exercising our power to make the client feel beautiful inside, we are really exercising our power over our own ability to become better at what we do and to improve the quality of our services to the client. The improvement in us, as well as the improvement in our services, cause both to become more valuable to the client, and more valuable services mean bigger profits, and more money in our pocket.

To do this, we simply lead the client from where they are to where we want them to be. If we have followed all of the other steps this is easy, because it is simply a matter of once again reversing the mirroring and matching process. Now that we are in deep rapport, they will follow us in the same way we have been pacing them: psychological reciprocity.

Additionally, people in rapport actually enter a light state of hypnosis, and consequently are more suggestible. Once we have established rapport with the client, they will be more susceptible to our suggestions, and the more susceptible they are to our suggestions, the stronger and deeper the rapport will become. In fact, the stronger and deeper the rapport, the more susceptible to suggestion the client will become. Thus, once we are in deep rapport it is merely a matter of telling the client exactly how they should feel, and they will generally accept all suggestions.

This is the phenomenon that we now utilize in reaching our desired goal of making the client feel beautiful inside. We also use it to exercise the power of influence and persuasion we now have over the client by virtue of the rapport we have built and the suggestibility that has resulted from it.

The process is the same for both persuasion and improving the client's state. With the client now in deep rapport, and consequently in a state of heightened suggestibility, we simply offer carefully and properly worded suggestions to them and they will tend to accept and follow these suggestions. They should be entwined with our normal conversation so they sound and appear very normal and natural, rather then standing out as some intentionally rehearsed script.

Before we study some sample suggestions, let us take a moment to review the process that has taken place in the client to whom the Mind Aesthetics® techniques have been applied to ensure that we thoroughly understand the internal processes.

As we learned in the *Human Mind* chapter, our mind can be conceived of as being divided in two parts: conscious and subconscious. We also learned that our conscious mind receives sensory input, and than compares it to our existing memories and experiences before criticizing the input and either sending it to our subconscious mind to be recorded and acted upon, or rejecting it, in which case it never reaches our subconscious. Additionally, we learned that our subconscious mind accepts any input it does receive as true, without analyzing it critically in any way. If for any reason information reaches our subconscious mind without being intercepted by our conscious mind, it will be accepted as fact and acted on accordingly.

When deep rapport is established through the application of the Mind Aesthetics® techniques (or in any other way), the client enters a light state of hypnosis. Hypnosis, by definition, is a state wherein the conscious mind and critical factor are bypassed and direct access to the subconscious mind is established. Once the client is in deep rapport (and light hypnosis), direct access to their subconscious results and any input they receive is accepted as true and acted upon accordingly. This is known as "suggestibility", since the input is accepted and followed without debate. If a client in this state is told that they feel warm, their subconscious mind accepts this as fact and they *do* feel warm.

Consequently, if the client in this state is told that they are relaxed, their subconscious mind accepts this input as fact and they will feel relaxed. If they are told that the massage feels deeper, their subconscious mind accepts this as fact and the massage feels deeper. If the client is told that the product you are applying will help their skin, they will accept that as fact, and be inclined to purchase that product if they want their skin improved. In addition, the product will be very likely to help their skin, as the subconscious mind will expect it to and use its power to improve the skin when the product is applied.

We can sum up simply how the process of Mind Aesthetics® works:

Mind Aesthetics® creates suggestibility in the client through the bypassing of their conscious mind, obtaining direct, unrestricted access to their subconscious mind, then offers suggestions directly to their subconscious mind.

It is important that you understand this process.

It is equally important that you understand its limitations: The subconscious mind has safety mechanisms in place, which will prevent the acceptance of any suggestion that is contrary to the client's morals, beliefs, or desires. Consequently:

No one can be made to do anything they would not normally do or they do not want to do.

With that said, let us look at some sample suggestions. *The Formulating Effective Suggestions* Chapter will offer instructions on how to properly word your suggestions.

The Magic

Some of the suggestions you might give include:

1. *"You know... it's interesting... whenever I relax ... like you are doing right now... I get a warm and fuzzy feeling inside that stays with me all day..."*

Suggestion one instructs the client that they are relaxed right now, that they will have a warm and fuzzy feeling inside, and that the feeling will stay with them all day. As you can see, suggestions are not overly complex - the simpler the better - and they need not be very direct. Making a suggestion such as "You will feel good" is unnecessary and would likely be ineffective. Remember that, although our conscious mind may have trouble understanding subtlety, our subconscious mind thrives on it and will very clearly and literally get the message of this suggestion. As a matter of fact, very indirect suggestions are often more readily accepted. Read the suggestion again. Now, imagine the value of having your clients feel "warm and fuzzy" all day, and attributing that feeling to your service. I am certain you would agree that eliciting such a response from your clients would be priceless!

2. *"Notice how good you feel while getting a massage? It penetrates right down to the core of your being ... Isn't that great?"*

If you were to give suggestion two to your client while you were giving them a massage, the massage would actually feel deeper. So deep, in fact, that it would reach the very "core of their being", wherever they imagine that to be. If you are a masseuse, ask yourself this question, "How many of my competitors are giving massages that penetrate to the core of the client's being?" My guess is none. Wouldn't it be wonderful if your clients were out there telling everyone they meet that you are offering such a massage?

3. *"It's nice to be able to get away ... like when you come here ... and turn off all the tensions of the day ... and just forget about them ... whenever you want to"*

Suggestion three is one of my personal favorites. In a wonderfully indirect way, this suggestion leaves three very important ideas in the client's mind:

1. When they come to your salon they get away from their tensions.
2. There, at your salon, they are able to turn off all of the stresses of the day.
3. They want to return.

It would not surprise me to learn that, if you gave this suggestion for instant relief from stress to your clients, many of them called for more than one appointment a week, perhaps even more than one a day!

4. *"Feel how the mask makes your face tingle, cleansing and rejuvenating your skin, it feels so good, and it is true that you can apply this mask yourself between your monthly appointments to have it professionally applied by me to keep your skin fresh."*

Suggestion four tells the client that she needs to purchase masks to take home while implanting the idea that she will return to the salon each month for you to apply the mask professionally.

5. *"The improvement you enjoy in your skin becomes even more desirable as you realize how easy the home regimen is for you to continue between visits here. That motivation to learn how to properly use the products is a reflection of how good you look!"*

Suggestion five serves several purposes. First, it suggests that the client perform the home regimen that you will suggest, thus encouraging the purchase of the product. Second, it ensures that the client will follow that regimen, making your job easier and more effective. Third, it instructs the client's subconscious mind that improvement is occurring (which her subconscious can actually make happen). Finally, it draws the client's attention to the improvements in her skin, and links that improvement to the proper use of the products you recommend.

When offering your client suggestions, think first of what you are intending to accomplish before you speak, and then formulate the suggestion completely in your mind before you say it. Suggestions can imply or actually state that what you are trying to accomplish is already done. For example, "Your skin *is* clear and smooth." This is useful as it has the effect of inducing the subconscious to make it happen because it believes it already has.

Your suggestions can also be of intended results, as in, "Improvements will happen." When using this method, it is always a good idea to put a time limit on the result, such as, "By the end of next month, the improvements will be complete."

17
Formulating Effective Suggestions

Proper suggestion formulation is essential to getting across the message you intend and having it followed. Remember that our subconscious mind does not distinguish between right and wrong, or between reality and fantasy, so we must exercise appropriate caution when making a suggestion and consider how it will be received.

First, let us study the three major types of suggestions we will use: direct, indirect and guided imagery:

Direct suggestions are authoritative in nature, for example, "You feel calm and relaxed."

Indirect suggestions are formulated in a more passive mode. Sometimes they even appear masked, "I wonder how good you will feel when I have completed your facial and you notice how calm and relaxed you are." Although it is never stated that the client will be relaxed, it is inferred, for it is impossible to accept the thought of how one will feel without accepting the fact that you have felt it.

Guided imagery uses the development of imagined or previously experienced sensory images to live or relive a scenario, "You see yourself ... in a beautiful field ... you are comfortable and peaceful ... it is the perfect temperature ... and the gentle breeze invites you become even more relaxed ... "

Different people will respond to each of these types differently depending on their representational type as well as a number of other factors. In my experience, however, most people will respond well to indirect suggestions, regardless of how they do with the other types, so if you are unsure which to use, use indirect.

Some people are natural story tellers, and if you are one of these, then you may find guided imagery more comfortable. Try different types and find what works best for you and which you are more comfortable using.

Direct suggestion, although the easiest to formulate, may sound intrusive to some people and should be used with care.

Regardless of the type of suggestions you use, they must conform to some guidelines. Below are the basic rules on how to properly word your suggestions for maximum clarity and effectiveness.

Speak Their Language

The first consideration in suggestion formulation is the client's dominant representational system. Just as in establishing rapport, we must communicate suggestions in the language the client speaks or they may not understand our meaning. Therefore we must keep the predicates of the client's dominant representational system in mind, and it is also useful to consider the individual client's speech patterns, as well as any other characteristics of their representational type. For example, for a kinesthetic we might word a suggestion to relax as:

> *"Feel yourself relax, as a warmth comes over your entire body, from head to toe, penetrating every muscle, soothing you."*

For the kinesthetic this suggestion would be spoken very slowly, in a somewhat monotonous voice. The same suggestion for a visual might be worded as:

> *"See yourself relax, visualize that relaxation as a warm glow, radiating through your entire body, bathing you in the warmth of its light, moving slowly through every muscle, illuminating you with comfort."*

For the visual this would be spoken in a faster, more expressive voice.

Be Positive

Well-formulated suggestions are positive suggestions. Remember, our mind only understands positive concepts, and negatives must be translated into positives first, before the uncertain process of rephrasing the negative does or does not take place. If a suggestion is formed negatively, it may not be followed, or worse, it may be understood as the opposite of what you were intending.

For example, this suggestion:

> *"You will have no tensions, no stress."*

could result in any one of three possibilities:

1) The client's subconscious mind could drop the negatives, rephrase the suggestion and understand what to do:

   "you will have [no] tensions, [no] stress."

   Then rephrase it as a positive:

   "You will have relaxation and calmness."

   accepting the rephrased, positive suggestion.

2.) The client's subconscious mind could ignore it completely because it is unclear.

3.) The client's subconscious mind could drop the negatives and understand what to do:

   "you will have [no] tensions, [no] stress."

   and skip the negation process and accept the suggestion as:

   "you will have tensions and stress."

Obviously, one in three odds of having your suggestion accepted as you intended are unacceptable. To avoid this, always phrase your suggestions as positive statements to ensure that they are more likely to be accepted and followed as well as being more likely to elicit the result you intended.

Be Literal

Our subconscious mind is literal, and it will take things literally. Thus we must inspect our suggestions and determine how the client's subconscious mind will understand them.

Consider this scenario: A client comes into your spa for a body treatment. You are able to observe that she is agitated and angry about something that happened at her place of work, and you want to improve her state. Carefully and properly, you use all of the Mind Aesthetics® techniques that you have learned, and quickly enter rapport with her and lead her towards feeling calm and relaxed. Now that she is in a state of heightened suggestibility and feeling better, you perform your service on her and offer suggestions to enhance the service and further improve her state. One of the suggestions you offer is, "It is interesting how, after your treatment today, you feel cool and calm all over for the rest of the day."

You complete your service and the client is noticeably calmer and feeling great. She thanks you for helping her feel so wonderful, and leaves the spa. For the rest of the day she feels calm, but she finds that she cannot seem to get warm, no matter what she does. She has a uncomfortable chill that lingers until she finally falls asleep.

Here is what went wrong: Your suggestion: "...you feel cool and calm all over for the rest of the day" was taken literally by her subconscious mind, and, in turn, it made sure that she was calm and cool (cold) for the rest of the day.

As you can see, it is crucial that you consider how your suggestions will be received and plan and adjust them accordingly. This is especially true of clichés which can have literal meanings that are quite different from their common usage. Think of how some of these clichés could be accepted by our subconscious mind:

> "No place like home" - Uncomfortable anywhere else.
> "The good old days" - All coming days are bad.
> "A sight for sore eyes" - Painful eyes when seeing the person in question.
> "Life is like a bowl of cherries" - My existence is as meaningless as a bowl of fruit.
> "Give it 110%" - This task at hand is clearly impossible for me to achieve.

Quite simply, you must avoid words with mixed meanings or those which may have some unique significance to the individual client (To a plumber a *pipe* is something you repair, to a tobacconist it is something you smoke, to a musician it is an instrument, to a seamstress it is an edging, and to a singer it is her throat).

Be Specific

Studies have shown that specific suggestions are more effective than very general ones.
For example:

> *"Notice how every muscle is relaxed."*

Would not be as effective in removing the tension in one's neck as:

Formulating Effective Suggestions

> *"Notice how the muscles in your shoulders have begin to relax, and that relaxation is spreading now, up into your neck, first one side, then the other and you feel the muscles in your neck become limp, like cooked spaghetti."*

When being specific, it is best to refer to the outcome you want to achieve as opposed to the method of achieving it. It is unnecessary to specify every little detail involved in reaching that outcome. Our subconscious mind will figure out the most efficient route - we just need to give it the destination.

Be Visual

A picture is worth a thousand words, or more, and visualization customizes the suggestion, as the client will realize it in their own way, from their experience and perspective. Determine what you want to suggest, and then verbally create a picture of that result. Use predicates and language that are suitable for the client's dominant representational system and create an appropriate scene.

For example, for a kinesthetic whom you are encouraging to return to have her make-up done for her wedding you might say:

> "Imagine how it will *feel* standing at the altar on the day of your wedding, your make-up, professionally done, *feeling smooth* and *comfortable*, still perfect even after the tears of joy *roll* down your face. You are confident that the whole bridal party will also be perfect even after the photos."

Be Realistic

It is important that your suggestions are attainable. Otherwise, the client's subconscious mind may simply reject them. For example, if you were to suggest that the client sprout wings and fly around the room, the suggestion will undoubtedly be rejected outright. Although our subconscious mind does not evaluate right or wrong, or the reality or fantasy of the suggestion, there is a built-in safety mechanism that prioritizes our subconscious mind's implementation of everything within its control. When presented with an outrageously impossible situation, it will discard it in favor of survival and self-preservation. That is, if the client were to fly around the room she would most likely fall and get hurt, so the attempt is simply not made. Consequently, make sure that your suggestions are well within the realm of the client's control, expectation, and belief of possibility of attainment.

18
The Mind Aesthetics® CD

The Mind Aesthetics® techniques are used when interacting with your client, to build rapport and provide an opportunity for you to introduce suggestions to persuade and influence the client, improve the quality of your service, and make them feel beautiful inside.

Now, suppose you want to automate that process, so that as you perform your service, your client's subconscious mind is opened and prepared and they are made to feel beautiful inside and out while their suggestibility is heightened. All of this is done without the need for you to say a single word.

Introducing The Mind Aesthetics® CD.

As I have already said, we treat the outside of our clients carefully and diligently using the latest products and techniques and utilizing all of our knowledge and skills. By doing so, we certainly do make them look as physically good as we can. That is our profession, it is what we do. However,

Make-Up Their Mind

that is only part of it. If we fail to treat the client's mind even the most excellent of services fall short of excellence.

Remember, the subconscious mind controls the muscles in the face as well as our conceptional sight. It is responsible for how we actually look as well as how we perceive our appearance. So, if the client does not feel beautiful inside they will not look beautiful no matter what - they simply cannot because, regardless of the effort we put into improving their external appearance, we cannot change the way they feel subconsciously with external services and products alone. On the other hand, if they feel beautiful at the deepest subconscious level, they will see themselves as beautiful and others will see that beauty also as their subconscious mind adjusts and modifies their external appearance to match their internal feelings.

This is why I developed The Mind Aesthetics® CD. We all know the power of using relaxing music in our salon or spa, how it soothes the client and helps put them in a relaxed state, preparing them to better receive the service we are about to provide.

Now imagine that this relaxing music has been carefully composed with patterns and tones that actually affect their alpha, beta and theta brain waves and causing their nervous system to experience an automatic calm, eliciting the physical and mental response of complete relaxation. That alone would be of great value to anyone performing a service or treatment to a client. However, add to that scientifically developed sound track carefully worded imagery guiding the client through a mind-journey of total relaxation. An all-encompassing physical and mental release of stress and tension. A complete relaxation of the body and mind, presented by a soothing, comforting professionally-trained voice that gently vocalizes carefully and properly worded suggestions that entice them into the deepest levels of relaxation, a wonderful state that many of them may never

The Mind Aesthetics® CD

have experienced before. Now, with the client open and ready, The Mind Aesthetics® CD actually applies a "treatment" to their mind, implanting genuinely beautiful thoughts and impulses, ideas of both literal, physical beauty and on a much deeper level, the subconscious understanding of the *concept* of being beautiful inside and out. Then, after their mind has been treated with the same care and excellence that you have applied to the outside of their body, they emerge with a uniquely intense feeling of well-being, instilled with an abundance of purely positive energy, a feeling of contentment that will stay with them, making them feel wonderfully beautiful on the inside as well as the outside

As you imagine the above scenario, you can begin to understand what The Mind Aesthetics® CD was created to do. Using relaxation hypnotics, The Mind Aesthetics® CD actually moves your client mentally out of the real world for a short time, taking them far away from the every day pressures, worries and tensions of their life, giving them an escape, a period of peace away from all of those unpleasant tensions. When they emerge and are brought back to the *real* world, something has changed. In addition to feeling beautiful inside and out, their attitude has changed and all of their problems and pressures and tensions somehow seem less overwhelming.

So powerful and positive is the client's reaction to The Mind Aesthetics® CD that many clients return to the salon or spa requesting Mind Aesthetics® to once again experience the intensely wonderful feeling they have when they emerge.

The Mind Aesthetics® CD can be used during facials, massages or wraps - any service that you offer - and when you use it, each service will become an entirely new and marvelous experience for the client when you apply aesthetics to their mind as well. The results are dramatic and exciting.

As satisfied clients spread the word your book can be filled with requests for services that include Mind Aesthetics®.

The Mind Aesthetics® CD also has the added advantage of working in compliment with the interactive techniques that you have learned in this book, or completely independently, without preparation of any kind. No training is required to use it. The results truly are amazing and you will be astonished at how client contentment quickly translates into an increase in referrals, repeat business, client satisfaction and compliments, all of which generates more and bigger profit!

However, we must also take a moment and recall our primary goal, that of making our client feel beautiful inside. Perhaps even more important than profit is the knowledge that you have really done some good for your client. You have improved the way they feel, their self image - you have improved their life. It is impossible to describe the satisfaction *you* will feel when your client emerges from the session and says, "Thank you! Thank you! This was the best I have felt all week! Thank you!"

The Mind Aesthetics® CD has been tested in the salon environment, and has received high marks, and only positive feedback. Its use is a study in simplicity. You simply play The Mind Aesthetics® CD and allow the client to listen to it during your normal service or even all by itself. I have heard of clients making appointments between scheduled appointments, finding reasons to return to the salon, just to regain the wonderful feeling that they received from experiencing The Mind Aesthetics® CD. Your clients will be thrilled with the benefits they gain from Mind Aesthetics®, and you will be equally pleased with how it helps to improve your bottom line!

The Mind Aesthetics® CD has been formatted to run for exactly one hour, with approximately forty-five minutes

The Mind Aesthetics® CD

of voice with music and a period of approximately fifteen minutes of music alone, so that you can adjust it to length of your specific service. This final period of music is also designed to allow you to offer your own suggestions directly to the client while their subconscious mind is still susceptible and prepared to accept them. You merely speak your suggestions directly to the client at any time during the final fifteen minutes as the music plays. You will also have a few minutes after The Mind Aesthetics® CD has ended to offer your suggestions, as the subconscious mind remains suggestible for several minutes after one emerges from the experience.

The development of Mind Aesthetics® represents an completely innovative approach to the field of beauty, and as we enter this unique era in the history of mankind, a time when people are suddenly becoming more aware and enlightened with respect to the needs of the mind and to how our mind effects our health, our well-being, our happiness, our field - the field of beauty - is also beginning to recognize the need to make our clients feel beautiful inside. Mind Aesthetics® automates the process, removing all the guess-work. Use it and I am certain that your clients will feel beautiful inside. Period!

See the order form at the back of this book for information on how to order The Mind Aesthetics CD®.

19
Ethics

I want to say a few words about the ethical use of The Mind Aesthetics® techniques and The Mind Aesthetics® CD. These techniques are designed to increase the suggestibility of the client for the purpose of enhancing their experience, improving the quality of the services they receive from you, and bettering the client's physical and mental state. They should be used as a compliment to the services you currently provide.

It is my belief that our subconscious mind is an intricate part of what we define as beauty, and it is my intention that these techniques be used only for the purpose of helping your clients. The very roots of Mind Aesthetics®, Hypnosis, NLP and Eastern Meditation have been around for centuries, all with the exclusive goal of improving the human condition and helping mankind. Mind Aesthetics® was developed with these same tenets in mind.

Once you begin to use Mind Aesthetics® the influence you will have over your clients is likely to increase greatly, and it is absolutely essential that you maintain the highest ethical standards when you use them. Our subconscious mind's primary goal is to protect us, and fortunately it will reject suggestions that it considers to be improper or inappropriate on any level. However, you should never test this. Doing so will permanently alienate you from the client.

If your goal in using The Mind Aesthetics® is anything other then I have mentioned, close this book and forget what you have read.

If, however, you are interested in improving yourself, your services, and your client's state, while increasing your business and profit, then we are on the same page, we are in rapport. In this case I am pleased to offer you the power of Mind Aesthetics®!

Appendix A

This appendix contains the self-hypnosis scripts used in the Sensory Acuity chapter to enter self-hypnosis while implementing the exercises. If you are interested in Hypnosis and wish to gain a better understanding of it, please get my book, "The Power Within: Unleashing Your Subconscious For Change", which contains complete, instructive study of the subconscious mind, hypnosis and NLP. For our purposes here, these scripts are presented to facilitate implementation of the exercises.

If you wish to tape these scripts for your personal use, at the end of this appendix you will find instructions for making a tape or CD for use in your exercises.

The dots [. . .] between the words in the scripts are intentional, providing a pause in the phrasing to create the proper patter in your voice. When you encounter them pause for two or three seconds

Relaxation Exercise

Before you begin the induction process, a relaxation exercise will help prepare your body for hypnosis. Slow, deep breathing elicits certain physiological changes such as a slower heart beat, relaxation of the muscles and the increase of circulatory activity in the extremities. All of these changes are conducive of the state of hypnosis.

Assume the comfortable position that you selected, ensuring that nothing is creating pressure anywhere on your body that could cut off circulation. Take a deep breath, breathing in slowly through your nose until your lungs feel completely full. Hold the breath while you count slowly to ten (about ten seconds), and then release it quickly. Feel your shoulders drop as your release the breath and your muscles begin to relax. Wait a few seconds (three or four) and take another deep breath through your nose, slowly filling your lungs until they have reached capacity, and hold it once again while you count slowly to ten. While you are holding your breath, think to yourself, "As I release this breath, all of the tensions in my arms and legs will be exhaled with the air." Release the breath quickly and notice how your entire body drops and becomes even more relaxed. Enjoy the feeling as you pause for a few seconds and then take still another deep breath, through your nose, feeling the fresh air fill your lungs completely. Hold it once again while you count slowly to ten, and as you are holding it, think to yourself, "As I release this breath, all of the tensions in my back and neck and everywhere else in my body will be exhaled with the air." Release the breath quickly as you notice the change in every muscle in your body.

You are now ready to proceed with an induction.

Induction Script - Progressive Relaxation

The progressive relaxation induction flows very smoothly and naturally as an extension of the relaxation exercise. In this induction, our conscious mind is involved in the physical process of relaxing the body, directing

Appendix A

attention away from external stimuli as well as from any concerns you may have about entering into the hypnotic state. You may use the words exactly as they are here, or you can change the format to the first person. For example, the statement, "*You* begin to feel the muscles in *your* legs relax," could easily be changed to the first person, "*I* begin to feel the muscles in *my* legs relax." When making a tape many people find that using the induction script in the second person is preferable, but either way is fine. Just use what works best for you.

The scripts presented below are written in the second person.

The progressive relaxation induction script follows:

"As you sit there ... so comfortable ... so relaxed ... close your eyes ...

and allow yourself to gently drift ... into a state of total relaxation ... you notice that you actually feel ... your body drifting ... more and more ... with each passing moment ... into a state of complete ... total ... relaxation ... want you now ... to focus all of your attention ... on your toes ... notice how each and every toe begins ... to feel heavy ... and drowsy ... and so comfortable . . . warm ... and relaxed ... and as you take a deep breath and hold it ... for a few seconds . . . until I tell you to release it . . . (*pause about five or six seconds*) ... now exhale quickly ... and begin to feel that warm . . . comfortable . . . relaxation moving down now . . . into your feet . . . and your feet begin to feel heavy . . . and drowsy . . . and relaxed . . . and it feels good . . . and the relaxation continues to move . . . moving into your ankles . . . and shins ... and calves . . . and you feel your ankles . . . and shins . . . and calves become heavy ... and drowsy ... and so relaxed ... you take another deep breath ... and hold it for a few seconds ... (*pause about five or six seconds*) ... and as you exhale quickly ... all of the tensions in your body leave with the exhaled air ... and you feel that warm ... comfortable ... relaxation moving up ... into your knees ... and thighs ... and hips ... as they become heavy ... and drowsy ... and relaxed ... and you notice that both your legs ... from your hips ... down to the tips of your toes ... are heavy ... and drowsy ... and relaxed ... feeling limp ... almost as if they are no longer there ... and you take another deep breath ... and hold it ... (*pause about five to six seconds*) ... and release it quickly ... exhaling even more tensions ... from your body ... and you notice ... the more you relax the better you feel ... and the better you feel ... the more you relax ... feeling wonderful ... better and better ... and you feel that warm ... comfortable ... relaxation move up even further now ... into your abdomen ... as you notice all of the organs in your abdomen ... feeling heavy ... and drowsy ... and relaxed ... and the warm ... comfortable ... relaxation moves up now ... into your chest ... into your shoulders ... and ... as you take another deep breath ... and hold it ... (*pause five or six seconds*) ... releasing it quickly ... you feel all of the tension in your shoulders ... leave your body as you exhale ... and your shoulders drop ... becoming ... heavy ... and drowsy ... and relaxed ... and the warm ... comfortable ... feeling of relaxation moves down your arms now ... slowly ... relaxing each and every muscle ... making your arms ... feel heavy ... and drowsy ... and so relaxed ... and it feels good ... as the warm ... pleasant ... comfortable feeling of relaxation ... moves down now ... into your wrists ... and hands ... and fingers ... to the tip of each and every finger ... as they

Appendix A

become heavy ... and drowsy ... and relaxed ... and you take another deep breath ... and hold it ... (*pause five or six seconds*) ... and as you release it ... you notice ... your fingers ... and hands ... and wrists ... are heavy ... and drowsy ... and so relaxed ... so relaxed ... it feels almost as though they are not there ... and you drift deeper and deeper ... into the relaxed state ... focusing within ... surprised and delighted with how wonderful you feel ... and that warm ... comfortable ... relaxed feeling moves now ... around ... into your back ... and ... as it travels down ... each and every vertebra ... one ... by ... one ... by ... one ... the relaxation radiates out to either side ... releasing all tensions ... removing all tightness ... as your back becomes heavy ... and drowsy ... and so very relaxed ... and that warm ... comfortable ... relaxation ... moves up into your neck ... and cheeks ... and jaw ... and you notice ... as your jaw drops ... and your teeth separate ... as it becomes heavy ... and drowsy ... and so relaxed ... and that warm ... comfortable ... feeling of relaxation ... moves further up now ... into your eyes ... and as you feel the movement in your eyes ... as they flicker ... or flutter ... or roll up inside your head ... becoming even more relaxed ... you notice your eyelids ... are so heavy ... and drowsy ... and so relaxed ... that they will not open ... even if you try ... they are stuck ... tightly shut ... relaxed and feeling good ... and you find ... the harder you try to open them ... the more difficult it becomes ... and the deeper you go ... as your eyelids are so heavy ... and drowsy ... and relaxed ... that they simply will not open ... and that relaxation moves further up now ... into your forehead ... and your forehead smoothes out ... as the worry lines disappear . . . and that relaxation . . . that feels so wonderful . . . continues now . . . moving to the back of your head . . . and up . . . up ... up ... to the very top . . . as your entire body becomes . . . heavy . . . drowsy . . . relaxed . . . and . . . as that warm . . . and comfortable . . . feeling of relaxation . . . moves . . . like a wave on the ocean . . . from the top of your head . . . to the tip of your toes . . . from the tip of your toes . . . to the top of your head . . . your entire body . . . is heavy . . . and drowsy . . . and so relaxed . . . drifting away . . . feeling as if it is not there . . . your limbs are limp . . . and loose . . . like a rag doll . . . or a wet cloth . . . and it feels good . . . and you feel good . . . as you go deeper . . . and deeper . . . and deeper . . . every word I say . . . causes you to go deeper and deeper. . . every breath you take . . . causes you to go deeper and deeper . . . each beat of your heart . . . takes you deeper and deeper and deeper . . . relaxing . . . drifting . . . feeling so wonderful . . . so comfortable . . .so warm and peaceful . . . better than you have ever felt . . . before in your life . . . and you take one more deep . . . deep breath . . . and hold it . . . (*pause about 10 seconds*) . . . and as you release it quickly . . . you will enter the hypnotic state . . . deeper and more completely . . . letting go . . . as you allow your subconscious mind . . . to take complete control . . . releasing yourself . . . wholly . . . completely . . . going deeper and deeper . . . feeling better and better . . . more and more . . . relaxed . . . "

Deepening Script - Counting Backwards

Counting backwards is an enormously effective way of redirecting our conscious mind, simultaneously increasing the depth of hypnosis. Mathematical thinking requires the

Appendix A

concentration and logic of our conscious mind. If the counting sequence is somewhat complicated, our conscious mind will quickly give up and retreat further.

This script can be modified to any numeric counting sequence that you find appropriate. Once again, moderately complicated sequences are better and provide quicker results, although care should be taken to avoid extensive mathematical calculations (for example, "count backwards in the square root of prime numbers"). Unless you are a math whiz, it is best to limit yourself to sequential counting such as the following:

"Take another deep breath... and hold it... (*pause five seconds*)... and release it... quickly ... feeling more and more relaxed... and take still another deep breath... and hold it... (*pause five seconds*)... and release it... quickly... as you go down *deeper* and deeper... and take one more deep breath... and hold it... (*pause five seconds*)... and release it... quickly... feel yourself sinking... ever deeper... into your hypnotic state... as it becomes ... everything you thought it would be... and take one last deep breath... and hold it... (*pause five seconds*)... and release it... quickly... as you breathe normally... the rhythm of your breathing... continues to relax you... taking you deeper and deeper... deeper into your relaxed state... and as you have relaxed your body... completely ... and continue relaxing... more and more... with each passing second... it is now time to relax your mind... in the same way... I want you now to begin counting... backwards... in increments of three... beginning with the number 300... as you count... picture each number... clearly in your mind... between each number... I want you to

155

Make-Up Their Mind

leave approximately 3 to 4 seconds . . . of time . . . time enough to inhale or exhale a deep breath . . . so . . . following this pattern . . . you will inhale on the first pause . . . and exhale on the second pause . . . inhale on the third pause . . . and exhale on the fourth pause . . . and so on . . . when I ask you to begin . . . you will count like this . . . 300 . . . inhale . . . (*pause four seconds*). . . and . . . 297 . . . exhale . . . (*pause four seconds*) . . . 294 . . . inhale . . . (*pause four seconds*) . . . 291 . . . exhale . . . and so on . . . you will find that as you count . . . each number will take you 10 times deeper and deeper . . . into your hypnotic state . . . deeper and deeper . . . more and more . . . with each passing moment . . . and your body . . . and mind will become . . . equally relaxed . . . as you count . . . an interesting thing will happen . . . after you have counted about 5 . . . or perhaps 12 . . . maybe even 15 numbers . . . you mind will become so relaxed . . . that you can no longer remember the next number . . . the numbers will just fade away . . . disappear from your mind . . . and when you are no longer able to see the numbers . . . just stop counting . . . and go even deeper into your hypnotic state . . . deeper and deeper . . . now begin counting . . . 300 . . . inhale and hold it for four seconds . . . (*pause four seconds*) . . . and . . . 297 . . . exhale and pause for four seconds . . . that's it . . . visualize the numbers . . . in your mind . . . inhaling and exhaling . . . as your mind becomes more relaxed . . . going deeper and deeper . . . 10 times deeper with each number . . . deeper and deeper . . . and soon the numbers will fade away . . . just disappear . . . as you go deeper and deeper . . . more and more relaxed . . . inhaling and exhaling . . . deeper and deeper . . . feeling better and better . . . letting go . . . letting go completely . . .

Appendix A

numbers fading away ... your mind is relaxing ... more and more ... and now ... if the numbers have not yet faded away ... make them go ... make them disappear ... as you go deeper and deeper ... more and more relaxed ... every breath ... every heartbeat ... every sound ... even the sound of my voice ... takes you deeper and deeper ... deeper than ever before ... and from this day ... now and forever ... each and every time ... you are ready ... and I suggest that you ... enter the state of hypnosis ... or the hypnotic state ... you will immediately ... reenter the hypnotic state ... and return to ... the depth you are now ... and go even deeper ... and deeper ... each time I suggest ... that you reenter hypnosis ... and you are ready to do so ... you will return to this level ... and go even deeper ... easily and quickly ... feeling better and better ... each and every time ... going deeper and deeper ... and deeper ...

Emergence Script

"In a few moments ... I will emerge you from your hypnotic state ... and when I do ... you will emerge feeling refreshed ... alert ... and wonderful ... you will feel rested ... as if you just had a full ... wonderful night's sleep ... and having awakened ... full of energy ... you will feel positive ... deep inside ... a feeling that everything is right ... and that feeling will grow ... and flourish ... and remain with you all day ... you will feel better than you have ever felt before in your life ... knowing that the work you have done ... is good ... and effective ... and will improve your life from this moment on ... I will count from one to five ... and when I reach five you will return to full conscious awareness ...

alert... awake and feeling great!... and now we start with one... beginning to come up... feeling that warm feeling that all is right developing deep inside... and... two... coming up a little further now... as you are starting to become aware of the changes in your breathing as we reach... three... and that wonderful positive feeling ... is growing stronger and stronger... you becoming even more alert as we reach... four... and that positive feeling is filling your entire being... you feel wonderful... better than ever before... and... five... wide awake... feeling great!"

Making A Tape

Making a tape recording of your induction scripts and suggestions can be beneficial on several levels. First, it allows you to completely relax and listen to the suggestions without the necessity of thinking about what you are going to recite to yourself next. For many, this gives them the freedom to delve even deeper into the hypnotic state. Secondly, once you have taken the time to make a complete and effective tape addressing your intended goals, you can replay it as frequently as you like, reinforcing the same suggestions without the concern of skipping some item. Lastly, once you become accustomed to the flow of the tape, you will develop the habit of entering the hypnotic state very quickly. The scripts presented in this appendix are written so as to be appropriate for taping.

A recording studio with specialized or hi tech recording equipment is unnecessary for making your self-hypnosis tape; any inexpensive cassette recorder will do. Today, many of us have computers with the ability to burn compact disks which work just as well. Any recording media

Appendix A

will do, you only need to be able to record and play back your script.

As I mentioned before, music can be used if you choose, although it is not required. If you do decide to use music, a simple way of incorporating it into your self-hypnosis tape is to have the music playing on a stereo or CD player at an appropriate volume behind you as you record your tape or CD. In this way, the microphone will pick up both the music and your speech, and they will blend together on the tape in the correct volume relationship to each other.

Self-hypnosis tapes should generally run for about thirty to forty-five minutes in length, depending on the length and complexity of what you are working on.

To make the actual tape follow these steps:

1. Locate the induction script, deepening script and emergence script in this appendix, and the exercise from the *Sensory Acuity* chapter.

2. Decide how you will incorporate the exercise into the tape (auditory acuity can be added to the tape, the others will require dead air on the tape to allow time to perform the exercise).

3. Read, practice and rehearse the induction and deepening several times until you are comfortable with the text and can recite it naturally. As you rehearse, be mindful of the tone, volume and quality of your voice and pay special attention to the patter.

4. Time your rehearsal to ensure that your tape will be an acceptable length. It is important that you maintain the rhythm throughout the entire session, avoiding the tendency to rush to fit more in. As a

rule, anything much more than forty-five minutes should be considered too long.

5. Make sure the room is quiet and free of all external noises. Pick a time of day when you will not be disturbed by the telephone or by other people in the house.

6. If you have decided to use background music, check the volume to ensure that it is soft enough so as not be distracting or so loud that your words cannot be heard.

7. Once you are comfortable with your reading of all the scripts you will be using, begin recording your tape, waiting for the blank leader to pass (about fifteen seconds), then start the music (if you are using it), and begin to read your induction. After about thirty seconds, stop the music and reading and rewind your tape. Listen to what you have recorded and make any adjustments necessary if it is not exactly right. For example, the music may be too loud, or you may be too close to the microphone, etc. If necessary, perform another thirty-second test until you are completely satisfied with what you hear.

8. With everything properly adjusted, rewind your tape to the very beginning, begin recording, wait the 15 seconds for the blank leader to pass then start the music (optional) and begin to recite your scripts, remembering to leave appropriate dead air for the exercise.

Appendix A

Once you have made your tape, and intend to use it for your session, I recommend the use of headphones to further exclude any environmental distractions. Get a pair of headphones that are comfortable and will not become annoying or begin to hurt during the session. Put the tape in the player and put the headphones on. Get comfortable and use the relaxation exercise to prepare your body for the hypnotic state. Once you have completed the relaxation exercises, press the play button and follow the suggestions on the tape.

Index

A

Aesthetics 1, 2, 3, 5, 35, 36, 37, 39, 40, 41, 43, 44, 58, 85, 92, 100, 104, 105, 111, 118, 124-128, 133, 134, 136-138, 141-145, 147, 148, 150-155, 167
Auditory 15, 26, 49, 50, 54, 67, 71-73, 76, 82, 83, 88-90, 93, 159

B

Bandler, Richard 1
Belief Systems 117

C

Calibration 121
Creativity 10

D

Death 24, 117
Desire 7, 37-39, 58, 117, 125, 128
Direct Suggestion 129, 133, 134

E

Emergence 31, 32, 33, 157, 159
Eye Accessing Cues 70, 74, 87

F

Fear 29, 45, 94
Feedback 144

G

Goals 39, 40, 63, 158

Grinder, John 1

H

Habits 10, 11, 100
Happiness 145
Health 7, 10, 145
Hypnosis 1, 30-33, 104, 126, 127, 147, 149, 150, 154, 157-159

I

Indirect Suggestion 129, 133, 134
Induction 30-33, 149-151, 158-160
Influence 2, 5, 11, 14, 35, 37, 39, 44, 58, 61, 65, 84, 85, 117, 120, 125, 126, 141, 147

K

Kinesthetic 15, 26, 29, 32, 50, 51, 54, 55, 67, 76-79, 83, 89, 93, 135, 139

L

Leading 105, 117, 118, 121, 122
Learning 64, 121

M

Memories 10, 70, 74, 78, 127
Mirroring and Matching 66, 97-100, 103-105, 107, 118-123, 126

163

N

Nature 38, 40, 76, 99, 133
Neuro Linguistic Programming (NLP) 1, 68, 147, 149
Non-verbal 29, 30, 64, 65, 97, 100, 117, 121-123

P

Persuasion 5, 26, 41, 85, 125, 126
Predicates 15, 70, 74, 78, 92-94, 109, 113, 121, 123, 134, 139
Profit 83, 126, 144, 148

R

Rapport 26, 34, 40, 44, 61-67, 91, 92, 97-100, 103-107 117-127, 134, 137, 141 148
Referrals 36, 37, 41, 66, 144
Relaxation 1, 3, 30-33, 40, 124, 135, 136, 139, 142, 143, 149-154, 161
Representational Systems 13-15, 26-29, 65, 67, 68, 70, 74, 81, 90, 100, 119

S

Script 64, 73, 75, 83, 92, 127, 149, 150, 151, 154, 155, 157, 158, 159, 160

Self Image 144
Self-hypnosis 30, 149, 158, 159
Sensory Acuity 29, 30, 44, 64, 119, 122, 123, 149, 159
Sight 14, 24, 49, 54, 68, 70, 79, 81, 104, 118, 138, 142
Sleep 11, 137, 157
Sound 11, 15, 17, 18, 20-26, 30, 31, 50, 54, 58, 68, 71-75, 82, 83, 88, 89, 100, 104, 127, 134, 142, 157
Stress 124, 130, 135, 136, 138, 142
Submodalities 27, 28, 29, 30
Suggestion 1, 35, 37, 39, 40, 41, 124-131, 133-142, 145, 148, 158, 161

T

Touch 17, 20, 32, 47, 50, 51, 54, 57, 73, 76, 77, 80, 83, 84, 89, 102, 111, 112

V

Verbal 29, 30, 34, 64, 65, 92, 94, 97, 100, 109, 113, 114, 117, 121-123, 139
Visual 14, 15, 18, 23, 26, 29, 30, 47, 49, 54, 58, 67-77, 79, 81, 82, 84, 88-93, 135, 139, 156

Bibliography

Alman, Ph.D., Brian M., and Lambrou, Ph.D., Peter. *Self Hypnosis*. Philadelphia: Bunner/Mazel, 1983.

Bandler, Richard, and Grinder, John. *Frogs Into Princes*. Moab: Real People Press, 1979.

Bandler, Richard, and Grinder, John. *ReFraming: Neuro-Linguistic Programming and the Transformation of Meaning*. Moab: Real People Press, 1982.

Blander, Richard, and Grinder, John. *The Structure of Magic II*. Palo Alto: Science and Behavior Books Inc., 1976.

Blander, Richard, and Grinder, John. *The Structure of Magic*. Palo Alto: Science and Behavior Books Inc., 1975.

Bretto Milliner, Charlotte. *A Framework for Excellence: A Resouce Manual for NLP*. Santa Cruz: The Center for Professional Development, 1989.

Brooks, Michael. *Instant Rapport*. New York: Warner Books, Inc, 1990

Dilts, Robert B.. *Applications of Neuro-Linguistic Programming: A Practical Guide to Communication Learning and Change*. Cupertino: Meta Publications, 1983.

Dilts, Robert B.. *Roots of Neuro-Linguistic Programming: A Reference Guide to the Technology of NLP*. Cupertino: Meta Publications, 1976.

Germain, Walter M.. *The Magic Power Of Your Mind*. No. Hollywood: Wilshire Book Company, 1956.

Goldburg, Dr. Bruce. *Secrets of Self-Hypnosis*. New York: Sterling Publishing Co Inc., 1997.

Gordon, David. *Therapeutic Metaphors: Helping Others Through the Looking Glass*. Cupertino: Meta Publications, 1978.

Hiatt, Ph.D, Marta. *Magic Mind - Techniques for Transforming Your Life*. St Paul: Llewellyn Worldwide, 2001.

Horton, Psy.D., William. *NFNLP Manual*. Englewood: William Horton, 1997

Kappas, John G.. *Professional Hypnotism Manual*. Tarzana: Panorama Publishing Company, 1987.

Krasner, Ph.D., A. M.. *The Wizard Within*. Irvine: American Board Of Hypnotherapy Press, 1977.

Kroger M.D., William S.. *Clinical and Experimental Hypnosis*. Philadelphia: J. B. Lippincott Company, 1977.

Maltz M.D., Maxwell. *Psycho-Cybernetics*. New York: Simon & Schuster Inc, 1960.

Mathes, L.. *Rapport: A Workbook*. Vienna: NLP of Washington D.C., 1982.

Minninger, Ph.D, Joan. *Total Recall - How To Maximize Your Memory Power*. New York: MJF Books, 1984.

Murphy, Dr. Joseph. *The Power of Your Subconscious Mind*. New York: Bantam Books, 1963.

O'Connor, Joseph, and Seymour, John. *Introducing NLP*. London: The Aquarian Press, 1990.

Rosen, Sidney. *My Voice Will Go With You*. New York: W. W. Norton & Company Inc, 1982.

Mind Aesthetics® CD
Order Form

Please send ___ Mind Aesthetics® CD @ $39.95 each
Florida Residents add 6% sales Tax: _____
Shipping & Handeling: _____
($3.50 US - $13.00 out of US)
Total: _____

Payment Method:
__Check   __ Money Order   __ Credit Card
(VISA, MC, AX, DIS)

_____ Ex Date ___/___

I agree to pay the above charges:

Signature:_____

Name:_____

Address:_____

City:_____State_____Zip_____

Send orders to: Dr. Julian Cauceglia
                     6385 Presidential Ct #203
                     Fort Myers, FL 33919
Phone Orders: (239) 481-5259
Online Orders: www.cauceglia.com
Email: julian@cauceglia.com

Mind Aesthetics® CD ISBN 0-9717407-0-4